THE

SOUL

SEVEN PRINCIPLES FOR PSYCHOLOGICAL AND SPIRITUAL WELLBEING

Dr. Nader Attalla
MD, CCFP(AM), ISAM, CSAM, Dip. Psych

Published by Dr. Nader Attalla
Calgary, Alberta, Canada
www.drnaderattalla.com
Email: admin@drnaderattalla.com
E-book ISBN: 978-1-7779903-1-2

Paperback ISBN: 978-1-7779903-0-5

Stylistic editing: Irene Kavanagh

Proofreading: Brooklyn Harrington, RSW

Reference editing: Melissa Vallieres, RN

About the Author

Dr. Nader Attalla is an Addiction Medicine and Family Medicine Specialist practicing in Calgary, Alberta, Canada, and a licensed Psychiatrist in Egypt. Dr. Attalla came to Canada in 2013 and has continued his medical education in the field of addiction medicine and family medicine. He is a clinical lecturer at the University of Calgary, teaching medical students and residents how to address a patient's physical, psychological, social and spiritual needs.

His experience in general and psychiatric medicine has provided patients with an increased awareness, of the importance of physical, psychological, social, and spiritual needs, as a measure of overall wellbeing. Dr. Attalla shares his knowledge and experience in both English and Arabic, at his clinic, on social media, and through scheduled talks, on the subjects of physical, mental, and spiritual health.

He has created "The Soul Program," with the help of other Calgary physicians and professionals, to help patients struggling with psychological difficulties and addictions. The program offers mental-health-awareness seminars, group-support therapy, individual counselling, and medication management. The focus is on seven spiritual principles that address struggles, with daily stress, as well as depression, anxiety, addiction, eating disorders, personality disorders, trauma, anger, and sleep problems. He wrote this book to provide a roadmap for spiritual wellness and to help unlock our innate capacity for happiness, success, health, love, and inner peace.

To my wife, our three beautiful children and everyone that has helped with the process and encouraged me to publish this book.

Contents

About the Author ---------------------------- 3

Foreword ---------------------------- 8

Chapter 1 - Introduction --------------------- 12

Chapter 2 - Non-Attachment ------------------- 30

Chapter 3 - Acceptance --------------------- 68

Chapter 4 - Non-Judgment ------------------- 79

Chapter 5 - Unconditional Love --------------- 93

Chapter 6 - Powerlessness ------------------- 114

Chapter 7 - Gratitude ----------------------- 124

Chapter 8 - Hope ---------------------------- 130

Comments ---------------------------- 145

References ---------------------------- 152

Foreword

Many people say that there is no physical health without mental health. I would suggest considering one step further and appreciate that there is no mental health without spiritual health.

I am a physician, specializing in Addiction, Mental Health, Chronic Pain and Occupational Health. I have spent my career in medicine, spanning over four decades, to explore and highlight health in context of biological, psychological, social and spiritual domains, despite my initial medical school training being very biological and pharmacological. Although I have taken time to explore all the major religions around the world, my interest in the spiritual domain is more based in physics, from the perspective that everything in our universe has the same basic building blocks of energy and matter; and the unified field in physics is reflected in individual and collective consciousness. I also have had opportunity to explore the ancient Indian source of all knowledge, Ved, that posits that each of us as an individual has a universal duty (Dharma) that is very personal in terms of meaning and purpose. In fact, the Ved is explicit in stating that each of us needs to discover and follow our own Dharma rather than following someone else's.

I have known Dr. Nader Attalla for several years in Calgary as a colleague and friend. I commend his efforts in undertaking this book to highlight the spiritual connections to better health. The ideas related to body-mind-spirit are also not new, but in our society today, around the world, there has been an over focus on the body at the expense of the mind often, with a frequent dismissal of the spirit among many circles that aim to be scientific. It is refreshing to see Dr. Attalla tackle this subject from the angle of seven spiritual principles that can be applied universally in our lives. His scholarly references in support of his theses will, hopefully, provide solace to those wanting some scientific foundations.

The human brain is biologically wired with our five senses to gather information about our surroundings. This information is interpreted further in the form of thoughts and feelings. Through our experiences with various interactions between our senses and our environment, we form attachments that feel desirable leading to pursuit of them; whereas others that feel undesirable often lead us to avoid them. Unfortunately, depending on what is or is not happening in terms of healthy brain function, the attachments that one would think promote health can become part of increasing ill-health. Avoiding some things that life offers for us to deal with compounds the problems. There is a common saying about this – whatever we resist persists – until we deal with it! Similarly, pain is an inevitable part of life with an injury, illness or things not going as one might expect; however, suffering is optional. In other words, suffering comes from the attachment to a particular outcome, which may or may not be real or changeable. Suffering is magnified with one getting stuck in victim or in being overly controlling to avoid certain circumstances. We have to remember that life is not what happens to us but what we do with what happens to us; as it is often not to us (personally) but rather it is for us to learn from and grow in awareness within ourselves and with others.

Expansion of awareness and healthy connection with others is needed to take an honest look at our attachments, judgments, thoughts and feelings that colour our interactions with ourselves on the inside and others on the outside. The quality of our relationship with ourselves and our inner dialogue has a direct impact on how we perceive people, places and things; thus, affecting everything from a very personal perspective. This can work to our advantage if all is functional and focused on health and well-being; however, it can work against us if our brain is giving us misinformation and/or it gets stuck in expectations, attachment to outcome and/or fighting to prevail, which is a common phenomenon among those who suffer with Addiction and Mental Health issues.

The seven spiritual principles that Dr. Attalla explores in this book are universal and can be applied in any context cross-culturally around the world. As much as hope and faith are discussed at the end, I hope the readers will take a circular view of these principles such that it would be helpful to begin approaching even the first principle of non-attachment with some hope and faith. Accepting the world as-it-is, rather than what we may think it should be, enhances our experience of it. It is only then we can choose to or choose not to engage in endeavours that are healthy or unhealthy for us and leave behind those that are potentially unhealthy and harmful to us and others. We need a lot of self-exploration in terms of love for ourselves and others unconditionally to find serenity and peace in our inner lives that can then radiate out. Love is truly a multi-faceted emotion that Dr. Attalla explores in detail in the chapter on unconditional love.

We all have innate interests and talents that we develop through our lives that serve us well if we are able to maintain perspective on what is and what is not in our control. We can invest in what we can influence and change only after we have a sense of the natural forces around us and have acceptance of what we cannot change. Most of all, everything that life brings our way needs to be accepted with gratitude. The blessings in life that we receive truly are grace from our Higher Power.

Through this book, Dr. Attalla encourages you, the reader, to take an exploratory journey that will help you discover your spirituality, your connection to a Higher Power, from a deeply personal and observer perspective. This is bound to further strengthen that connection within you and around you with others, especially if you already have had a spiritual connection from previous work from other perspectives.

I am grateful to be invited to write this foreword, as an appetizer to interest you and inspire you to explore the real you for better spiritual and mental health. I wish Dr. Attalla and all the readers of this work, who will apply these seven principles in their lives, all the best for an honest spiritual journey that will bring lasting inner peace and contentment.

Dr. Raju Hajela

MD, MPH, CCFP (AM), FCFP

Consultant - Addiction Medicine, Mental Health and Occupational Health

President and Medical Director of Health Upwardly Mobile Inc.

Clinical Professor, Cumming School of Medicine, University of Calgary

CHAPTER ONE
Introduction

~ Why I Wrote This Book ~

My patients, students, and colleagues remain the inspiration behind this book. After observing significantly positive changes in my patients, I felt motivated to gather my thoughts on spirituality. My colleagues reported that the principles, shared during group therapy and educational seminars, provided a roadmap to our innate capacity for happiness, success, health, love, inner peace, and creativity. These principles are useful for all dimensions of wellbeing: physical, emotional, social, and spiritual. They help people struggling with daily stress, depression, anxiety, addiction, eating and personality disorders, trauma, anger, and sleep issues.

Initially, I was reluctant to write a book about spirituality, as it is seen by many as a controversial topic. Nonetheless, when looking at studies and evidence, it has demonstrated an encouraging impact on mental and physical health. The World Health Organization (WHO) has highlighted the importance of a spiritual dimension in health. When viewing individuals, using a whole-person approach, biological, psychological, social, and spiritual aspects are equally important to our wellbeing, and it is by addressing these levels simultaneously that we can more successfully maintain optimal health and recover from illness.

Although there are genetic factors that affect our overall health, epigenetic signals from habits and environment could have a considerably greater influence. Therefore, we must choose wisely and understand that it also takes intention and dedication to maintain our overall health. As individuals, we need real whole foods, movement, relaxation, plenty of rest, fresh air, sunshine, a positive mindset, and community.

We also have spiritual needs, such as the need for hope, meaning, purpose, the need to feel connected with ourselves, nature and others. Ultimately, we have the need to be loved. These spiritual basics become more prominent during times of sickness and suffering as several studies have shown. [(1)]

Before I delve further into spirituality, I would like to first mention the most important areas needing attention, when addressing physical, psychological, and social needs. Greater strength can be developed through their advancement, with each element acting to reinforce the other.

***

PHYSICAL NEEDS

Regular exercise, sleep hygiene, healthy diet, medication if needed.

Regular exercise/physical activity

Why exercise/engage in physical activity?

Exercise benefits go far beyond the physical (better sleep, less physical pain or physical illness). It also offers psychological and emotional benefits. Regular exercise can aid in releasing feel-good endorphins, as well as natural brain chemicals, like those found in cannabis, which can enhance our sense of wellbeing.

Physical activity has been shown to benefit a variety of mental-health conditions and issues, including depression, anxiety, eating and bipolar disorders, schizophrenia, addictions, grief, relationship problems, dementia, and personality disorders. In addition, physical movement is associated with enhanced mood and energy, reduced stress, deeper relaxation, improved mental clarity, learning, insight, memory and cognitive function, enhanced intuition, creativity, assertiveness, and an enthusiasm for life. Exercise and physical activity are among the most important things we can undertake for mental, physical, and general emotional wellbeing. [2-4]

How much is enough?

Studies have shown that daily exercise, of thirty minutes or more, can significantly improve emotional disturbances, with as little as ten to fifteen minutes of movement, making a positive impact. Some of my patient's favorite activities include walking, yoga, dancing, gardening, Tai Chi, lifting weights and organized sports.

How to stay motivated

Choose an activity you enjoy doing and invite a partner, co-worker or friend, to join you. Begin to incorporate these activities, as part of your lifestyle, with a focus on personal improvement, rather than viewing it as something "I need to do." Think about what might be stopping you from exercising or being physically active, and you will likely find a solution. Whatever the reason—lack of energy, not having the money to spend on sports, being too busy with young children or your job—there is always a way to overcome it. For example, if you have a restricted budget, do something cost-free, like walking in nature, or involve your children and spouse and make it part of your family's quality time together. It will also help to set reasonable goals. Think realistically about what you are able to do and begin gradually.

Sleep Hygiene

The amount and quality of sleep you get has an astonishing impact on health maintenance and mental wellness. Sleep is the time when the body repairs itself. Hormones are produced during the night (e.g., melatonin), which are necessary for the immune system and recovery from daily stresses. Poor sleep weakens your body defenses as well as the process of repair. Our internal biological clock, or circadian rhythm, serves to coordinate internal time with the external world. Studies show that if the circadian rhythm is not properly synchronized with the twenty-four-hour solar day, it can lead not only to an increased risk of physical disease but psychiatric illnesses, including depression.

If you have difficulty sleeping, or wish to improve your sleep, try the following tips: [5-6]

1. **Follow a sleep schedule**

   Everyone has personal sleep needs. On average, adults need seven to eight hours of sleep, per night. Going to bed and getting up, at the same time each day, helps with this, as limiting variations in your sleep schedule, to no more than one hour, will ensure that you maintain a healthy circadian rhythm. If you don't fall asleep, within approximately twenty minutes, leave your bedroom and do something relaxing, like reading or listening to soothing music. Go back to bed when you're tired and repeat, if necessary.

2. **Create a restful room**

   Keep your bedroom cool, dark and quiet. Consider using darkening shades or a sleep mask. Minimize blue light from electronics directly before bedtime. Artificial light from lightbulbs, TV screens, computers, and smart-phone screens interfere with melatonin production and prevent you from sleeping. Set aside at least thirty minutes before bedtime to unplug and prepare for sleep. Calming activities such as a warm, Epsom-salt bath, soothing music, reading, drinking valerian or chamomile tea, and deep-breathing exercises or other relaxation techniques may promote better sleep.

3. **Avoid stimulants**

   The stimulating effects of nicotine and caffeine take hours to wear off and can disturb your quality of sleep. While alcohol may make you feel sleepy, it can disrupt sleep later in the night. Additionally, in terms of optimal sleep, it's best not to go to bed too hungry or too full.

4. **Avoid daytime naps**

   If you choose to nap, limit the time to twenty or thirty minutes and avoid doing so late in the day; otherwise, it could interfere with your nighttime sleep.

5. **Exercise during the day**

   Regular physical activity can improve sleep, but try to avoid too much exercise, too close to bedtime.

6. **Manage your worries**

   Meditation, journaling and breathing exercises can help with managing stress and controlling anxiety.

Healthy and balanced diet

Many chronic illnesses, including mental and behavioral problems, are exacerbated by modern diets. Evidence continues to mount, linking chronic diseases with modern foods, yet these conditions can be helped and even prevented, by eating a diet of nutrient-dense whole foods, i.e., the foods our ancestors ate, such a fresh, non-processed, and farm to table foods.

Here are easy-to-follow tips:

Eat whole foods in the form that Mother Nature made them. *Choose real food over processed food.* ***Consider adding fermented foods to your diet.*** *(e.g., kimchi, lacto-fermented pickles, sauerkraut, kefir, yogurt, kombucha, etc.)*

Whenever possible, choose foods that are grown locally.

Eat foods in their proper season.

Choose pesticide- or chemical-free, GMO-free foods.

Studies have shown that certain types of foods can cause chronic inflammation. Long-term inflammation occurs without symptoms inside your body. This type of inflammation can trigger illnesses like diabetes, heart disease, fatty liver, cancer, and mental illnesses, such as depression and anxiety. We know from research that some foods cause inflammatory and other negative effects on mental health, while some produce anti-inflammatory effects and have a positive impact on mental health. [7]

Consider minimizing these inflammatory foods:

Refined carbohydrates/flour: White bread, white pasta, pastries, chips, pretzels, crackers, cookies, pastries, etc.

Processed sugar (cane sugar and corn syrup): Candy, soft drinks, sugar-sweetened drinks and fruit juices, cakes, cookies, doughnuts and certain cereals, etc.

Processed vegetable/seed oils and trans fats (partially hydrogenated oil): Margarines, butter replacement, vegetable and seed oils such as corn, canola, peanut, sunflower, grapeseed.

Other processed foods: Highly processed red meat (e.g., hot dogs), fast foods/fried foods or anything in packaging that may contain inflammatory foods, such as white flour, sugar, and hydrogenated/vegetable oil.

Alcohol: *It is best to abstain from alcohol, especially if you have mental-health problems.*

Consider adding more of these anti-inflammatory healthy foods:

Fatty fish**:** Salmon, sardines, mackerel, etc.

Whole grains: Oatmeal, brown rice, whole-wheat bread

Nuts and seeds: Almonds, walnuts, pumpkin seeds, etc.

Vegetables: Garlic, onions, mushrooms, cauliflower, bell or chili peppers, green leafy vegetables such as spinach, broccoli, Brussels sprouts, kale, etc.

Fruit: Tomatoes, pomegranates, deeply colored berries (grapes, cherries, blueberries, etc.)
High-fat fruits**:** Avocados and olives

Chocolate: Dark chocolate and cacao

Healthy oils: Olive oil and coconut oil

Spices: Turmeric, ginger, cinnamon, etc.

Tea: Green tea

PSYCHOLOGICAL

For emotional wellbeing, we need to focus on identifying and processing our emotions through journaling, daily affirmation, and talking to others who will not judge us. These could be a close friend or family member, or someone found in counselling through individual and group sessions

We should also practice behavioral techniques aimed to promote a relaxation response: Meditation, mindfulness, breathing exercises, guided imagery, progressive muscle relaxation, etc.

Learning CBT skills (cognitive-behavioral therapy) and DBT skills (dialectical behavior therapy) have shown tremendous impact on mental health, as CBT and DBT are powerful tools, that promote new patterns of thoughts, feelings, and behaviors and are rooted in evidence-based practices, for treating different mental illnesses.

SOCIAL

"No Man is an Island." ~ John Donne

Community is one of the most critical elements of wellness and healing. No one can go through profound transformation alone. We need each other to thrive and recover. Mutual support through the twelve-step groups such as Alcoholics Anonymous (AA) or any other support group, are an immensely powerful healing space, where we can find inspiration in our recovery journey, by communicating with others. You can also find community within holistic and spiritual groups, local yoga groups, permaculture, school, work, through volunteering, and so on. In so many ways, our health is linked to our experience of connection with others. Research tells us that social isolation leads to physiological and psychological struggles.

SPIRITUAL

When I asked my patients why they think spirituality is important, or rather, what they get from spirituality, these were their responses:

- Feel supported and not alone.
- Feel peace, love, and joy
- Discovery of my true self
- Find meaning in life and personal values
- Feel a sense of purpose
- Release of control to a higher power
- Expand my support network while getting to know others who have similar interests

When I asked my patients how they establish spiritual connectedness, they provided me with the following examples:

- A sense of connectedness to self, others, nature, or a higher power.
- Spending time in nature
- Meditation, contemplation, prayer
- Ceremonies
- Creativity
- Group gatherings
- Helping others
- Twelve steps of AA
- Religion
- Painting, dancing, singing, playing instruments
- Writing poetry

Difference between religion and spirituality

Dr. Harold Koenig, psychiatrist in the Faculty of Medicine at Duke University, has undertaken the first systematic evidence-based analysis of the connection between mental disorders and religion, and illustrates the difference between religion and spirituality. [(1)]

Religion

Religion involves beliefs and practices related to the *transcendent*, wherein the transcendent is God, Allah, or a higher power in Western religious traditions, or to Brahman, Buddha, or ultimate truth in Eastern traditions. Religions have specific beliefs about life after death and rules about conduct within a social group. Established religious traditions can be practiced in private or public settings.

Spirituality

Spirituality is the connection to that which is sacred, or the *transcendent*, which can be outside of, and within, the self. Spirituality can be achieved through religion or can extend beyond organized religion. It includes a search for both the transcendent and the discovery of the transcendent, through which you discover your true self, find meaning in life, and feel a sense of purpose.

Carl Jung's views on spirituality and mental health

Most mainstream psychotherapies have largely ignored the spiritual dimension of our being with the exception of the holistic, or whole-person, approach such as Jungian analysis and transpersonal psychology. The purpose of most psychotherapy is to adjust the ego, for which there is often no conception of what lies beyond it. In contrast, a transpersonal approach proposes that there are developmental stages beyond the adult ego, which involve experiences of connectedness with the self, others, nature, or a higher power. Carl Jung, the Swiss psychiatrist and founder of analytical psychology, was recognized as a leader in the field of transpersonal psychology by calling attention to the importance of spiritual experience. He suggested that psychological development extends to include higher states of consciousness and can continue throughout life, rather than stop with the attainment of adult ego maturation.

Unlike Sigmund Freud and his followers, who described religion as an obsessional neurosis, Carl Jung considered the psyche as a carrier of truth, powerfully rooted in the unconscious mind. He suggested that there is a spiritual instinct in all human beings, an inherent striving toward a relationship with someone or something that transcends human power—a higher force or being. He agreed that spirituality and its practices, such as rituals and dogmas, were necessary to protect the human psyche when coping with stress and suffering as it has throughout human history. In his work, he also stated that if there were no religion, human beings would create one. He wrote that without a God, or higher power, humans would make a god out of something—money, sex, power, political movements, stone, or reason itself.

According to Jung, both religious practice and religious experience found their source in the collective unconscious. In one of his letters, he wrote, "Buddha's insight and the incarnation in Christ break the chain of suffering through the intervention of the enlightened human consciousness which thereby acquires a metaphysical and cosmic significance." (Carl Gustav Jung letters, Volume II, P. 311)

Research on spirituality and mental health

As mentioned earlier, spirituality has a positive impact on mental health. Below, I will share some information, from studies, that have shown the correlation between spirituality and mental health.

Spirituality is associated with major physical health benefits, like greater longevity and immunity. Additionally, it may even reduce the risk of many chronic conditions and is one of the keys to psychological wellbeing. It provides resources for coping with illness and other stressful life changes, enhances positive emotions, and helps neutralize negative emotions, which, in turn, reduces the likelihood that stress will result in emotional disorders, such as depression, anxiety, suicide, and substance abuse. Let's look more closely at some of the major research collected from *Handbook of Religion and Health* by Dr. Harold Koenig. [1,8]

Coping with stress

Several studies have revealed that spirituality helps people cope with life stressors, especially those involving medical or psychiatric illness. These studies report that spirituality was helpful in dealing with medical illness, chronic pain, caregiver stress, psychiatric illness, grief, end-of-life issues, natural disasters, war and acts of terrorism, and other adverse life situations. [9]

Positive Emotions

Expression of spirituality is associated with an increased level of positive emotions, such as wellbeing and happiness, hope and high self-esteem, and a sense of purpose. It provides an optimistic worldview that may involve the existence of a higher force (God) that loves and cares about humans and is responsive to their needs. It also allows one to release control over events and situations. Spirituality provides answers to such existential questions as, "Who am I?" "Where do I come from?" and "Where do I go from here?", thus reducing existential pain, by normalizing loss and change.

In addition, human virtues are encouraged in many spiritual traditions, including love of others, compassion, kindness, gratitude, forgiveness, and they may directly enhance positive emotions and buffer stress. [(10-19)]

Depression, suicide, anxiety

Research findings report a lower level of depression or faster recovery among those who practice spirituality. In a recent study, spirituality correlates with neuroanatomical changes, specifically cortical thickness in the brain. [(20)] Other studies show that there is less suicide, fewer suicide attempts, and generally more adverse attitudes toward suicide among those who are religious or spiritually involved. Studies also reported significantly reduced anxiety among those who are more spiritual and those receiving spiritual guidance. [(21-24)]

Addiction

Spiritual involvement is related to less alcohol and drug use. It has also been shown to help people recovering from alcohol and drug addiction. There is now an emerging number of studies that show health advantages and the recovery benefits of faith-based programs such AA, or twelve steps. [(25-27)]

Social problems

Spirituality also provides practical morality along with a set of ethics and guidelines for behavior and values. Indeed, research shows that spirituality reduces the likelihood of delinquency and crime. Furthermore, spirituality and religion encourage altruistic acts such as helping others and emphasize a focus outside the self. This may increase positive emotions and serve to distract from one's own problems. It is associated with greater marital stability and satisfaction as well as a lessening of spousal and child abuse. [(28-29)]

The Negative side of religion and spirituality

There are times when religious and spiritual teachings can be harmful. It is said there has been more bloodshed in the name of God than for any other cause. The following are examples of religion's negative impact:

- Interpretation of the scriptures can sometimes lead to hatred, aggression, prejudice, and the exclusion of others; gaining power and control over vulnerable individuals; encouraging judgment toward others and encouraging intolerance against minority groups.
- If religion is based on the fear of sin, rather than on the love of God, it can lead to anxiety, fear, and excessive guilt.
- Religion may also encourage magical thinking, like treating God as a genie that responds to our personal wishes.
- Failure of physical healing may trigger frustration and distress.
- Religion may be used instead of medical care. For example, individuals may delay investigations and treatment to "demonstrate their faith."
- Some religious teachings resist the development of modern science.

While the effects of religion and spirituality can be negative; it is still generally associated with greater wellbeing, improvements in coping with stress, and better mental health. (8,30) That is to say, don't discard something undesirable, along with something valuable, or, in other words, don't throw the baby out with the bathwater.

Include spirituality in health assessments

Since many patients have spiritual needs or turn to spirituality, to regain hope and meaning in times of illness and pain, health-care professionals should include the following recommendations in their practice: (30)

- Knowledge of the patient's spirituality or religious beliefs. This will help create some context, around how one or both influence our understanding of disease and its correlation to the healing process.
- Acknowledge the worth and benefit of the patient's faith and traditions.
- Ascertain the spiritual wishes and needs of the patient.
- Are these spiritual wishes and needs being met?

I find using these questions, in my assessment, helpful in understanding individual's spiritual background:

- What gives meaning to your life?
- What values are important in your life?
- Do you believe in a higher power?
- Do you have a personal relationship with your higher power?
- Can you describe your spiritual belief system?
- How are your spiritual needs met?
- Can you describe your experience with religion?

What kind of spirituality is good for mental health?

I've spent a few years of my practice, in Canada, questioning my patients who practice spirituality and asked them what they like most about their religion, beliefs and traditions. After some years, it was evident that what they appreciated about their religion was almost the same. I began writing what I had been told and combined it with research and studies, which then manifested into the book you're reading now. I was interested in finding out if similar concepts had been investigated before. My conclusion was that the main spiritual principles, that help people psychologically, are the same seven I summarize below, which underscore the intention of the book.

1. **Non-Attachment**

   Non-attachment means being "OK with or without" the things surrounding us. Trying not to feel too attached to such things as money, position, titles, physical appearance, and so on. Valuing everything and becoming attached to none of it. It is important to remember that we were not created to possess but rather "to be with."

2. **Non-Judgment**

   Experience the present moment with neither indifference, attraction, nor revulsion. Practice seeing things as they are without judgment, including toward yourself, others, or life experiences. None of us has the capacity to know everything.

3. **Acceptance**

   Accept others, knowing that people would do better if they could.

   Accept yourself—we cannot change anything until we accept it.

   Accept life—try not to resist it but rather work with it.

4. **Unconditional Love**

   Practice loving yourself, others, and all forms of life—everywhere and under all conditions, without exception. Most important, balance between loving yourself and loving others.

5. **Powerlessness**

   Admit that by yourself (ego/self), you are powerless over many things in life, and that a power greater than you is necessary to return to a state of love, joy and peace. This power beyond you can be called the universe, nature, energy, consciousness, God. Names do not matter.

6. **Gratitude**

   Be grateful for all that you have and seek to honour all life experiences, whether or not comprehensible or pleasant. Appreciate the positive experience; see the negative experience as a learning opportunity.

7. **Hope and Faith**

   Never lose hope or faith. Remember that at the end, everything will work out for the best. Holding positive goals in your mind is inspirational and helpful, because what you hold in your mind tends to manifest in reality.

These principles are crucial to psychological wellbeing and studies, I will share, have revealed their importance. When medical residents and physicians, as well as psychotherapists and counsellors include these principles, in other psychological interventions, such as dialectical behavior therapy and cognitive behavior therapy, they can result in more positive outcomes.

I believe that applying these principles, in the preparation and integration of psychedelic experiences, during psychedelic-assisted psychotherapy, will increase positive emotions such as joy, love, peace, and a sense of unity and oneness with the universe and with others, in addition to lowering guilt, depression, anxiety, and fear. Several studies have found that psychedelic-assisted therapy can lessen PTSD and fear of death, in terminally ill patients.

All of these principles have also aided patients struggling with personality disorders and addiction problems, especially those in search of meaning in life and those who are undergoing existential crises.
They will help parents willing to fulfil their children's spiritual needs and atheists seeking spiritual connection, without involvement in organized religion and dogma.

This book offers help to religious leaders and spiritual teachers who are interested in understanding spirituality from a different perspective.

Origin of the principles

The first form of life, which could have originated some four billion years ago, looked like bacteria. These organisms were able to replicate/reproduce as separate entities. Single cells have evolved into the current diverse, complex organisms we see today, including minerals, plants, animals, and humans.

Animals and humans acquired what was needed from the environment in order to survive. This is somewhat different from plants, which have chlorophyll that uses sun as a source of energy. Animals, by instinct, knew they must conquer and compete with other organisms for survival. They developed curiosity and intelligence through evolution and continued to evolve into progressively higher life forms.

With the cognitive revolution of approximately seventy thousand years ago, our ancestors developed larger brains and better ways to communicate through gestures and language. Gradually, human beings have become the most powerful force on Earth, from east Africa across the globe, through expanded and stored knowledge and collective learning. We still, however, possess part of the primitive reptile brain that focuses on survival and feels separate from other organisms, humans, and nature. Although all forms of life emanate from the same source, and we are all interconnected, the idea of separation has never left us since the earliest forms of life. We do not feel one with each other or with nature. Our animal instincts have evolved psychologically, to make us feel separate and different. We can feel hate, fear, and anger toward other human beings. We began to over attach to things around us, believing that attachment will guarantee immortality. We began to resist life with all our power, while trying to control everything. We learned to judge ourselves and others, thinking that judgment will save us. Based on our survival, we instinctively learned to love but only with conditions that we place on others.

It is my belief that these principles will counter and eliminate negative behaviors and emotions felt, towards ourselves and others and, consequently, benefit our mental health. Practicing non-attachment, acceptance, non-judgment, unconditional love, powerlessness, gratitude, and hope and faith will help restore our harmony with nature, our oneness and connectedness with surrounding life, with God, and other human beings. I believe that our evolution will continue; not simply as physical evolution, but more so a psychological and spiritual movement forward, from Homo sapiens to Homo Spiritus. In other words, from our survival-driven, ego self-centeredness to higher forms beyond ego. In doing this, we will continue to evolve beyond our ego, to what we call our highest virtues, as expressed in the seven principles.

***

CHAPTER TWO

NON-ATTACHMENT

Everything in this world is transient, and loss or change is inevitable. Spiritual traditions, in their wisdom, tell us, it is our ignorance or resistance to impermanence that generates attachment and, consequently, suffering, psychological pain, and fear of death. If we are governed by worldly things, which are fleeting in nature, we will continually resist the flow of life. Loss or change will then draw us back into negative emotions such as anxiety, depression, and grief.

Michael A. Singer, author of *The Untethered Soul* writes, "Life is continuously changing, and if you're trying to control it, you will never be able to fully live it." Our mind tends to control life experiences, through clinging to and avoiding what we perceive as being desirable or not. It is then, in surrendering our worldly attachments, that we can experience happiness and be present in the moment.

This is the biggest and most significant chapter in the book, as I believe that non-attachment is the main principle, among the seven.

WHAT IS NON-ATTACHMENT?

Non-attachment simply means "to be OK with or without," or free of worldly attachments, whether it be an object (car, house, etc.), a person, our own bodies, thoughts, emotions, and even life. In this state, we are no longer controlled by desire or attachment, by the ego. We can fully engage in life experiences with flexibility and without fixation on the outcomes. In other words, we can simply enjoy a thing without depending on it for personal happiness. We can see that the source of happiness is from within (Self) and, thus, there is no longer fear of loss or change. Again, non-attachment is a path rather than an event. It takes practice and time to develop this wise virtue, as we are seeking progress, rather than perfection.

The highest spiritual path is freedom from attachment and aversion. Non-attachment has been taught as the way to enlightenment; it is a central teaching in many faiths, such as Buddhism, Christianity, Islam, Hinduism, and Taoism. It is now found in forms of therapy: Cognitive Behavioural Therapy (CBT) and Dialectical Behavioural Therapy (DBT), which emphasizes the ability to become detached from thoughts.

STAGES OF PSYCHOLOGICAL AND SPIRITUAL GROWTH

You can meditate or contemplate while using the concepts below, which may help you develop an attitude of non-attachment. The more you practice non-attachment, the greater your resilience to life-changing events or losses.

The stages of spiritual growth help us arrive at the question, "Who am I?"
The first step in spiritual growth is coming to know that you are not the materialistic possessions you own (money, house, car, work, position, title, or degrees).

The second step is in the understanding that you are not your body. You are not the physical beauty that you may have nor the physical illness you may suffer from.

The third step, a stumbling block for many, is the realization that you are neither your thoughts nor feelings. You are not the ideology held in your mind, nor are you the mental positionalities, models, or plans that you set. You are not the preconceived ideas, or the conditionings absorbed from society. You are not the physical desires nor the sexual orientation that you identify with. The intent of meditation is pure detachment, from the notion that thoughts are "mine" or "me."

Ultimately, you recognize that you are well beyond that. As you arrive at the heart of the question of who you truly are, you will discover your authentic self [Buddhist Self, Christian Soul, Hindu Atman]. Beyond your ego, with its endless collection of memories, you will find there is greatness within and feel open to the presence of self/God. This is the highest level of psychological and spiritual growth.

Saints and sages of all religions have guided us to ask: Who am I? Who sees what I see? Who feels what I feel? Who dreams what I dream? Who thinks what I think? Descartes' answer: "I think, therefore I am." The truth is that you are *not* your thoughts; you are the one aware of your thoughts. You exist regardless of thoughts. "You are not defined by what you do or what you have. You are the one who is building the building." If you go to the depth of the questions, "Who am I?" "Is there something in me that will never die?" (e.g. your soul, spirit) you will discover that beyond the ego/mind, there is a place of pure silence, unconditional, and eternal. A way to experience this pure silence and infinite love within is by practicing meditation and contemplation. I believe such ideas can lower anxiety and fear, encountered by those facing terminal diseases, such as stage-four cancers, when they realize that death is not the end. Studies have shown that psychedelics used for providing therapy, for terminal cancer patients, are helpful tools to facilitate the understanding of this idea.

Buddhism and Non-Attachment

In Buddhist tradition, all things in this world are subject to change and loss, and with attachment to worldly phenomena comes suffering. Buddha realized that the pathway to enlightenment is via non-attachment and he discovered the Four Noble Truths. Those four truths teach that experiencing suffering is an inevitable part of existence; suffering arises from attachment to impermanent things; suffering ceases when attachment ceases, and freedom from suffering is possible by following the Eightfold Path.

THE FOUR NOBLE TRUTHS:

1. ***Suffering***
   Life involves suffering; we always feel an undercurrent of anxiety and uncertainty inside.
2. ***The Cause of Suffering***
   Ignorance of impermanence leads to over-attachment (craving, desire), and, therefore, causes suffering when we encounter or anticipate loss.
3. ***The End of Suffering***
   Suffering ceases by letting go of over-attachments/desire toward things.
4. ***The Path***
   Freedom from suffering is possible, by following the Buddhist Eightfold Path (e.g., non-attachment, compassion, meditation, mindfulness, etc.).

Christianity and Non-Attachment

Monotheistic religious traditions have taught us that it is better to detach from worldly things, with the emphasis on attaching to the divine or God instead. When God become one's primary source of attachment (indeed, the first commandment in Judaism, Christianity, and Islam), everything else is secondary.

Jesus' basic teaching was non-attachment: *to be in the world but not of it. The kingdom of God is within you.* He taught us not to attach or identify with that which is transitory and awaken ourselves to what is eternal, unconditioned, and unchanging within—our true nature. In Christianity, the material world is not an illusion; it is a temporary level of reality, as we're only on the earth for a short time. The illusion is our perception, our attachment to this physical body/ego or to that which is impermanent. Nothing in this world of decay is destined to last forever; *everything that has a beginning has an end.* So why be attached to what is impermanent? In biblical terms, attachment is "idolatry of matter," meaning to allow something relative to take the place of the Absolute, or God. Idolatry of matter gives rise to our pain and suffering. *As we look not to the things that are seen but to the things that are unseen. For the things that are seen are transient, but the things that are unseen are eternal.* (Corinthians 4:18)

To realize the impermanence of all things can reduce attachment to and possessiveness toward worldly things. *From now on those who have wives should live as if they do not; those who mourn, as if they did not; those who buy something, as if it were not theirs to keep; those who use the things of the world, as if not engrossed in them. For this world in its present form is passing away.* (Corinthians 7:29-31) These words remind us that our happiness and our suffering are equally impermanent: *this too shall pass*. Sickness, in terms of identification, can be seen as transitory. If you were diagnosed as having depression, perhaps, instead of labelling yourself a depressive; you are able to see that the disorder does not define who you are. *You are not a depression, you have a depression. You are not a sickness but rather the subject of it.* A person can better live with a condition without identifying with it. It is the way we see our sickness that makes the difference. The idea is not to go into detachment or indifference, as this will lead to the path of negation. Suffering is not an illusion; the agony of humankind is real.

The parable of the Prodigal Son is another example of the lesson of non-attachment (Luke 15:11-32). A father has two sons, the younger of whom asks for his portion of the inheritance, from his father. This son, however, is wasteful and extravagant, and he squanders his fortune. He returns home empty-handed, intending to beg his father to accept him back as a servant. His father welcomes him with celebrations. The story illustrates how we seek to fulfill our happiness with things of the world, when true happiness comes from within.

Detachment (Indifference) vs Non-Attachment

In your spiritual practice, it is important to understand the difference between detachment and non-attachment. Detachment can lead to indifference, passivity, avoidance, apathy, or loss of interest in life. By contrast, non-attachment does not require the renunciation of life, like moving to the caves of the Himalayas. Rather, it involves simply participating fully in life without attachment to the outcome, doing whatever would normally drive you, but without fixation and worry about the outcome. Non-attachment is an aspect of love, and it connects you to the world and people around you.

Is Love Possible Without Attachment?

There is often the misunderstanding that love is an aspect of attachment. The truth is that as you move toward it, you will see that true love is free of attachment, dependency, and possessiveness. You clearly see that others do not belong to you; they are free beings and to love them is to respect such freedom. You love them without feeling over-attached or dependent on them, for your happiness; you are "OK with or without" that person. Therefore, you first need to feel complete within yourself; otherwise, you may seek that lack of love in others. In a healthy relationship, you complement each other rather than complete each other. Sometimes, it is better to remove yourself from a relationship that repeatedly causes emotional disturbances, due to over-attachment, codependency, or abuse. This means you can walk away, out of love for yourself. If you become over-attached and feel you cannot live without that person, to such a degree that you must control them, this will create suffering, as everything is subject to change and loss. Again, non-attachment is the key to a happy relationship without codependency, control, possessiveness, and jealousy, and it will greatly help you practice interdependence.

Secure Attachment vs Non-Attachment

Non-attachment is closely related to secure attachment, although the two are distinguishable. People with a history of secure attachment are less likely to cling to, or grasp, at life. In secure attachment (the psychological term in accordance with attachment theory), a person feels confident when a partner or caregiver is nearby. In attachment theory, babies and children need to feel this bond with their mothers and fathers in order to develop a mature ego. Secure attachment is the building foundation of a mature ego. One needs a mature ego first, to more easily advance to non-attachment later in life. Carl Jung wrote, "The first half of life is devoted to forming a healthy ego, the second half is going inward and letting go of it."

Benefits of Non-Attachment and the Middle Way

Reducing fixation on the need for the experience to be one way or the other brings more peace and inner joy. The Taoist quote, *the flow of life is neither sought nor resisted*, means that "I will be OK whether or not it happens; I let the river flow as it is." In this state of non-resistance, one is non-attached to events or worldly phenomena. This is not indifference; one fully participates in life without being run by it.

Buddha tried to give up all attachments, by leaving his community, friends, and family, to meditate in the forest, with wise men. He eventually discovered that this extreme path was not necessary, nor did it made him any closer to enlightenment. He recommended the middle way by avoiding the extremes, meaning giving up over-attachment and over-avoidance.

St. Augustine said, "I sat on top of the world when I came to fear nothing and desire nothing."

By living with non-attachment, we have less fear of loss and change, allowing us to cope with the uncertainty of life and this can greatly reduce our emotional disturbances. Studies have shown that it reduces symptoms of depression, anxiety, and stress.[1-2] Instead of spending time and energy focusing on fear of loss, we become more mindful of the present moment.

Non-attachment is also an aspect of true love and the key to healthy relationships. Studies show that non-attachment increases pro-social behaviours, such as empathy and kindness.[3] This will help us avoid unhealthy or toxic codependent dynamics.

An attitude of non-attachment can bring us to advanced psychological development and self-actualization.[2] Individuals who went through near-death experiences have reported a peaceful feeling of oneness and connectedness. These experiences were reported from those able to let go of attachment to ego/body.

Studies have shown that when attachment to God or a higher power is secure, religious involvement is associated with better mental health. On the other hand, when one's attachment to God is insecure, it may have the opposite effect on mental health.[4-5]

EXERCISE:

1. *What areas of your life do you feel over-attached to?*

2. *What benefits can you get when you practice non-attachment?*

How to Practice Non-Attachment in Self-Esteem, Relationships, Parenting, and Past Trauma

Non-Attachment in Self-Esteem:

Self-esteem is multidimensional, a term to describe a person's overall sense of self-worth. The need for self-esteem plays an important role, in psychologist, Abraham Maslow's, hierarchy of needs. Maslow suggests that people need self-esteem in order to grow, as a person and achieve self-actualization.

Self-esteem relies on many aspects of our lives. There is physical, performance, social, personal, and religious self-esteem. Everyone defines and identifies with certain dimensions of self-esteem. We may ask ourselves the question, "How do I define myself and what positive things do I have in my life?"

Any attachment or fixation on the self-concept, whether positive or not, can be problematic, due to the ever-changing nature of experience. If an individual clings to positive notions of self, such as being a "high performing student," then receiving a poor mark on an exam challenges this positive view.

Being non-attached toward self (ego), which includes self-concept, allows us to move with the flow of life with greater flexibility. Otherwise, life changes will be perceived as a threat to self-esteem.

Again, it is essential to have self-esteem to allow development of a mature and healthy ego. But there is no need to over-identify with self-esteem dimensions. Over-identifying with our physical appearance, physical health, assets, qualifications, goals, family, and so on, we become prone to emotional suffering, as everything is subject to change and loss. Over attachment to our children will trigger fear of loss and might trigger over-protection, control, and possessiveness, which will have a negative impact on children's development. We must remember that nothing belongs to us, and that we enter the world with nothing and will leave with nothing." Strong attachment may also block us from getting what we want. Strong desire or over-identifying with any aspect of self signals to the universe and others all that we don't have, which could become a self-fulfilling prophesy in terms of remaining unable to get it all.

Dimension of Self-Esteem

1. **Physical self-esteem**
   Self-esteem based on physical appearance and physical and intellectual ability.

2. **Performance self-esteem**
   Self-esteem based on work performance (money) and academic performance (high IQ).

3. **Social self-esteem**
   Self-esteem based on relationships with people such as family members and significant others.

4. **Personal self-esteem**
   Self-esteem based on personal traits (e.g., kindness, courage, generosity, easy-going).

5. **Religious self-esteem**
   Self-esteem based on religious practices and traditions.

The core of most emotional disturbances is fear of loss generated by our ego attachments and identification. If we practice non-attachment, even to self-concept, we may experience more peace, love, serenity, happiness, and enlightenment. We are born with nothing, and we leave with nothing.

Non-Attachment in Relationships

Practicing Non-Attachment in Relationships: Set boundaries

Being non-attached doesn't mean being detached from others. It means you value your relationship with yourself as much as with others. Set clear boundaries with partners, family, and friends so that you have both respect and space. Learn to say no at times, and ask for what you want to maintain the relationship

When you set boundaries with others, you can express how you feel in unpleasant circumstances and explain what has generated your feelings. Avoid accusatory words, which leads others to believe that you are placing blame, otherwise this could immediately provoke their ego-defence mechanism. Communicate in a way that doesn't cause people to feel threatened. The art of using a loving, communicative tone in your relationship takes time and dedication.

Spend time without your partner

There is no need to feel obliged to call or text throughout the day! Hang out with friends, on your own. Don't feel the need to be with your partner or friends every day. Plan time alone for self-reflection and the processing of your feelings.

Let them go if they want to leave

Never beg someone to be with you. Do not allow yourself to be abused or used, only to try and please someone who wants to leave.

Compromise when you don't agree

Avoid trying to make someone else always see and do things your way. Let go of your need to control their actions. Instead, find areas of compromise to accommodate you both, and strive to find common ground all the time.

Classic Compromise Solutions from Dialectical Behavioural Therapy

- **I'll cut the pie; you choose the first piece**

  Mary divided the artwork into two groups following their divorce: Peter chose his preferences.

- **Take turns**

  Peter prefers the mountains, but Mary wants the beach for their vacation. Their decision is to alternate between them both.

- **Do both—have it all**

  Peter wants dinner, but Mary decides on a movie; they make the decision to do both.

- **My way when I'm doing it; your way when you're doing it**

  Each person exercises their own method in handling problems.

- **Tit for tat**

  I'll clean the bathroom once a week, if you dust and vacuum every week.

- **Trial period**

  Agree to a solution for a specific length of time, then reassess.

- **Split the difference**

  Mary wants to vacation for ten days, but Peter prefers to go for five. Their decision is to meet in the middle and vacation for seven days.

Practice unconditional love (Agapē)

Practice loving yourself, others, and all forms of life, everywhere, without exception or conditions. Agapē is the highest form of love and is free of attachment, possessiveness, and dependency. It will be discussed further, in a separate chapter.

EXERCISE:

1. *Out of the dimensions of self-esteem, noted above, which one are you afraid of losing, and how would you cope if it happened?*

2. *Give examples of how to come up with comprises for current or past problems*

   Conflict:

   Compromise:

   Conflict:

   Compromise:

Non-Attachment in Parental Love

Parents often navigate between conflicting recommendations, they hear, on how to raise babies and children. Some parents respond to the caution, against kissing and cuddling their offspring, whereas others will follow the extreme application of "attachment parenting," which encourages parents to hold and cuddle their infants all the time, never leaving them alone, not even to sleep. The question could be: what is the most effective parental style? An authoritative parental style is perhaps the answer. The truth is that both tactile and loving human contact, along with a safe and structured environment, is necessary for normal emotional and physical development.

This means providing affection and structure, along with freedom, to develop as an independent human being. To allow this freedom, it is essential to practice non-attachment in parenting where a child's needs are responded to without demanding anything in return. Allow them to explore their world as much as they safely can given the level of maturity at that moment. Teach them without demanding that they agree with you on everything. In this way, the child will feel accepted and free to follow their personal life path.

According to psychologist Diana Baumrind, there are four parenting styles based on two dimensions: control (structure) and affection (love and warmth).

1. ***Authoritative parents***

   Authoritative parental style is the most effective, because it balances both structure and affection. It allows the practice of non-attachment, by respecting a child's freedom according to the level of maturity. Parents who exhibit this style listen to their children and provide love and warmth in addition to structure (discipline). They are assertive, but not intrusive nor restrictive; they avoid punishment and threats, instead relying on strategies such as positive reinforcement. This approach to parenting is equally demanding and responsive. Each child is encouraged to develop a unique and innate potential.

   Outcome: Children of authoritative parents tend to have high self-esteem, high grading in education, high academic achievement, high social skills, conflict resolution skills, set boundaries, and show less involvement in drug abuse.

2. ***Permissive***

   Permissive parents provide more affection than structure. They are more responsive than they are demanding. Usually, children run the show and parents play the role of a friend, rarely using punishment or confrontation and allow considerable self-regulation.

Outcome: Children tend to have reasonable social skills, but low academic achievement. They are more involved in risky behaviours such as alcohol, drugs, unprotected sex and gambling.

3. ***Authoritarian parents***

   Authoritarian parents provide more control than affection. They are highly demanding and directive, rather than responsive. Bedtime is bedtime. There is no communication, and providers expect their orders to be obeyed, without explanation and their beliefs and traditions followed, without explanation.

   Outcome: Children of authoritarian parents tend to succeed academically, but not socially and psychologically. These children are often distant and passive and struggle with repressed negative feelings, such as guilt, fear, hate, and anger, all of which can cause anxiety and depression.

4. ***Uninvolved parents (neglectful)***

   Uninvolved parents are low in both control and love. They are indifferent and not responsive to their children's needs, nor would they respond to basics needs such as shelter, water, and food.

   Outcome: Children tend to perform poorly in all domains (academic, social, and psychological); they are more anxious, socially withdrawn, exhibit a lack of assertiveness and are vulnerable to abuse and addiction.

Healthy parenting involves healthy attachment, providing love, independence, and structure.

EXERCISE:

1) *What was your family parenting style and what was the impact on you?*

2) *How would you practice the authoritative parenting style with your children?*

Let Go of Attachment to Past Experience: Healing the Past

Understanding Trauma, PTSD and C-PTSD

What is trauma?

Before we discuss letting go, of the effect that trauma has, and how to practice non-attachment to past experience, we need to fully understand its effect on us.

Emotional trauma is the result of any stressful or terrifying events, witnessed or experienced, that shatter our sense of security. It is not the nature of the event that makes it traumatic. Rather, it is the subjective emotional experience that defines an event as traumatic or not. Thus, the more frightened we feel, the more likely we are to be traumatized. Most people who experience trauma may have a temporary difficulty adjusting and coping, but with time and self-care, they usually recover. If the symptoms get worse, last for months, and interfere with daily life, the result may be PTSD or C-PTSD.

Traumatic experiences may include the following:

One-time event: a major accident, injury, or a violent attack.

Ongoing stress: life-threatening illness, bullying, or domestic violence.

Social media and news: terrorist attack, plane crash, or mass shooting. Viewing these images over and over can cause severe anxiety.

Other causes: surgery, the sudden death of someone close, or a breakup.

A landmark study entitled ***The Adverse Childhood Experiences (ACE) Study*** was done on 17,000 participants and found that a significant relationship exists, between the number of traumatic experiences that occur early in life and negative outcomes later in life. Participants who were victims of emotional, sexual, and physical abuse, physical and emotional neglect, household dysfunction, such as mental illness, substance abuse, and domestic violence, were found to have greater risk for many behavioural, physical, and mental health issues in adulthood. These issues include smoking, alcohol abuse, lack of physical activity, drug abuse, missing work, multiple sexual partners, sexually transmitted diseases (STDs), adolescent or unintended pregnancy, depression, suicide attempts, severe obesity, diabetes, chronic lung disease, stroke, cancer, and heart disease.

Post-Traumatic Stress Disorder (PTSD)

Another complication of trauma is PTSD, a mental-health condition, typically triggered by a short-lived trauma or traumas of limited duration.

Symptoms of PTSD may include the following:

- **Reliving the traumatic experience:** trauma is re-experienced through memories, nightmares, or flashbacks.

- **Avoiding certain situations:** large crowds or driving, that remind you of the traumatic event.

- **Physical symptoms:** these refer to physical symptoms that don't have an underlying medical cause. For example, you might feel pain, muscle tension, IBS, dizziness, etc.

- **Changes in beliefs and feelings about yourself and others:** this includes negative emotions, such as guilt and shame toward yourself or bitterness and anger towards others. You might not be able to trust others or the world.

Complex Post-Traumatic Stress Disorder (C-PTSD)

On the other hand, C-PTSD, according to the International Statistical Classification of Diseases (ICD-11), is a prolonged, repeated experience of trauma, most often the result of childhood shock. This can include chronic sexual, psychological, and physical abuse and neglect, chronic intimate partner violence, victims of kidnapping and hostage situations, victims of slavery and human trafficking, prisoners of war and concentration-camp survivors. People with C-PTSD share the symptoms of PTSD mentioned above; however, they may also report the following issues:

- **Attachment (insecure):** problems with relationship boundaries, lack of trust, social isolation, and difficulty perceiving and responding to others' emotional states; altercations in relations with others (isolation and withdrawal) or a repeated search for a rescuer.
- **Biology:** sensory-motor developmental dysfunction, increased psychosomatic symptoms, increased medical problems.
- **Emotional regulation:** poor emotional regulation, difficulty identifying and expressing emotions and internal states, and difficulties communicating needs, wants, and wishes, chronic suicidal preoccupation, compulsive or extremely inhibited sexuality.
- **Dissociation:** amnesia or reliving experiences, depersonalization, and impaired memory for traumatic events.
- **Behavioural control:** problems with impulse control, aggression, and sleep disturbance.
- **Cognition:** problems with planning, judgement, initiation, difficulty processing new information, difficulty focusing and completing tasks, and language developmental problems.
- **Self-concept:** disturbed body image, low self-esteem, excessive shame, sense of helplessness or paralysis of initiative, sense of being different from other human beings.

- **Changes in perception of the perpetrator(s):** preoccupation with revenge, idealization, a sense of a special or supernatural relationship with a perpetrator, and acceptance of a perpetrator's belief system.

EXERCISE:

What is the emotional and physical impact of a rough upbringing?

How We Let Go of Past Trauma:

There are multiple trauma-focused therapies, such as Cognitive Processing Therapy, Prolonged Exposure Therapy, Eye Movement Desensitization and Reprocessing Therapy, Art Therapy.
We will review some of the non-attachment skills that help with trauma therapy.

Letting go and forgiveness to overcome anger and resentment

Forgiveness is the decision to let go of negative emotions toward yourself, others or events. Forgiving others enables you to let go of anger, resentment, and bitterness. When you forgive yourself, you can let go of guilt and shame.

If you experience injustice or pain, inflicted by another person, you have the option to hold bitterness within you or to forgive. Forgiveness allows you to release yourself from negative emotions. Once they are acknowledged, you can choose to dismiss them, offering them up to a cosmic judgement or a higher power. Forgiveness is a continuous process of replacing negative effects with acceptance, peace, empathy, and compassion.

True forgiveness is the state of understanding the other person and the reasons for their behaviour, so clearly, that you can truthfully say there is nothing left to forgive.

Again, to forgive with the heart can take time, and it's an ongoing process.

There are two types of forgiveness:

- **Decisional forgiveness:** Keeping negative emotions, while forgiving. (Mindful forgiveness)

- **Emotional forgiveness:** Changes in feelings toward the offender, as you forgive and release yourself from all internal negative feelings. (Heartfelt forgiveness)

The desire to heal from past experience involves freeing yourself from resentment, bitterness, and other negative feelings. Essentially, you need to move towards emotional forgiveness. While decisional forgiveness may reduce hostility, it is not sufficiently effective in improving stress levels or emotional health.[6]

What forgiveness is not:

- It is not approving, denying, or overlooking negative behaviour.
- It is not simply moving on.
- It is not forgetting or pretending nothing occurred.
- It is not the justification or letting go of possibly needed justice.
- It is not bargaining or negotiating.
- It is different from reconciliation, which requires a sincere apology from all parties.
- It is not dependent on the one you forgive, thereby transferring power to another, to control and keep you in bitterness.
- It is not a restoration of full trust (trust takes time to develop or be reinstated).

THE FOUR PHASES OF FORGIVENESS, ACCORDING TO COGNITIVE BEHAVIORAL THERAPY:

The Uncovering Phase

You improve your understanding of the injustice and how it has impacted your life.

The Decision Phase

You make the decision to choose or reject forgiveness, as an option.

The Understanding Phase

You start to understand the offender in a new way, which will allow positive feelings toward the offender and you.

The Meaning Phase

You may find meaning in the experiences and see the negativity as a learning opportunity.

Uncovering Phase

During the uncovering phase of forgiveness, your understanding of the injustice, and how it has impacted your life, will improve.

EXERCISE:

Describe the injustices in your life. What happened?

How have the injustices affected you?

- Painful emotions (anger or shame)
- Changed behavior (avoiding new relationships)
- Practical costs (time or money)
- Changed worldview ("people are evil")
- Cognitive rehearsal (recurring thoughts about injustice)
- Physical harm (injuries from abuse)

What feelings do you have towards the offender?

Decision Phase

During the decision phase of forgiveness, you will gain a deeper understanding of what forgiveness is and make the decision to choose or reject forgiveness, as an option.

EXERCISE:

What are the pros and cons of deciding to forgive the person who caused you difficulty?

Pros:

Cons:

Describe how things might be different, if you decide to forgive.

The Understanding Phase

During this phase, you seek to understand the offender, which may initiate compassion.

What was life for the offender like, as they grew up (parents, environment, neglect, abuse, genetic influence)?

What was life for the offender like, at the time of the offense?

List the feelings you currently have toward the offender, after reflecting on these points.

The Meaning Phase

During this phase, you may find meaning in the experience and recognize ways in which you have grown, as a result. You see that a life crisis can be an opportunity for growth or resentment, for forgiveness or hate, to learn or to grow discouraged.

The theory of Logotherapy, developed by psychiatrist Viktor Frankel, was founded on the belief that human nature is motivated by the search for meaning. Frankel's theories were influenced by his personal experience of suffering and loss, in Nazi concentration camps. In Frankel's book, *Man's Search for Meaning*, he wrote "Everything can be taken from a man, but one thing: to choose one's attitude in any given set of circumstances.

EXERCISE:

Describe how you have grown, and what did you learn from this experience?

Writing a Forgiveness Letter

Writing a forgiveness letter can be a powerful tool to heal past wounds. It may take time, as it is different for everyone. You are not sending the letter to the offender, but you may share it with a counsellor or someone you trust. The goal is to let go of negative emotions. The letter will consider the same points we discussed earlier.

Include the following in the forgiveness letter:

- These were your chosen actions:
- Here is how they have impacted me and my daily life:
- Here is how their enduring presence affects me:
- If I can find forgiveness, here is how I envision better managing my life:
- Here is how I have come to understand your actions:
- Here is how I see forgiveness, as the best way forward:
- Here are the clearest points I have taken and learned, from all that has happened:

EXERCISE:

What have you learned from past negative experiences? Are you willing to forgive, and, if so, how?

Research on Forgiveness

Research reveals that greater forgiveness and forgiveness interventions are associated with less stress, anxiety, depression, and other negative emotions, as well as overall better mental health. It is also associated with improved satisfaction with life, fewer physical ailments, better sleep quality, and reduced fatigue.[7-11]

A study looked at twenty psychologically abused and divorced women, who were randomized between forgiveness therapy (FT, based on the Enright model) and an alternative treatment (AT, anger validation, assertiveness, interpersonal skill building). The study found that the FT group showed a greater improvement in forgiveness, self-esteem, state anxiety, trait anxiety, depression, environmental mastery, finding meaning, post-traumatic stress symptoms.[(12)]

Identify and Replace Trauma Related Negative Core Beliefs

Identifying specific core beliefs, caused by past trauma or negative experiences, is an important part of recovery, as these are what shape how we respond to life situations. It isn't easy to identify and change these core beliefs, however it's important to remember that while core beliefs feel true to us, that it doesn't mean that they are. You may say, "I feel like such a loser," but these feelings don't reflect the truth. Consider labelling beliefs simply as beliefs, rather than accepting them as true facts about yourself. Keep an open mind and recognize that misrepresentations can indeed feel true.

The following is a list of the most common negative core beliefs, as a result of trauma:

- **Helplessness:** The belief that you can't cope with a particular situation or with life in general.

- **Worthlessness:** The belief that you are unworthy or of no value.

- **Failure:** The belief that you aren't good enough, or can't do anything right.

- **Unlovable or Unlikable:** The belief that you are impossible to love, that no one cares about you, and that you can't make or keep friends or experience a romantic relationship.

- **Abandonment:** The belief that significant others will leave and that being alone is intolerable.
- **Mistrust:** The belief that others are untrustworthy, leading to a state of paranoia.
- **Vulnerability:** The belief that you are unsafe (relationally, medically, financially) or overly susceptible to being hurt.
- **Emotional inhibition/repression:** The belief that you must inhibit your emotions as others will not understand them.
- **Emotional deprivation:** The belief that you will not get your emotional needs met within a relationship.
- **Entitlement:** The belief that you are special, or, in some way, better than or more deserving than others. Narcissism is often a cover for insecurity.
- **Punishment:** The belief that you deserve to be punished.
- **Insufficient self-control:** The belief that you have no self-control, no ability to restrain yourself or delay gratification. This leads to impulsivity and addiction.

EXERCISE:

What are the negative core beliefs that you usually struggle with, and how would you change them?

Non-Attachment and Letting Go of Past Errors (Forgiving Yourself)

Difference between Guilt and Shame

Guilt and shame are closely connected emotions. We tend to feel guilty when we believe we have violated rules that are important to us or when we have not lived up to the standards, we have set for ourselves. Shame fosters a sense of our being "flawed," "no good," "inadequate," "rotten," "awful," or "bad."

Based on cognitive therapy and the twelve-step program, here are some questions and skills, to help us let go of guilt and shame.

1. **What is the full measure of the damaging action(s)?**

   The following questions should be asked to weigh the severity of your actions:

   - How do others' judgement of my actions compare with the extent of my guilt?
   - How will I view my responsibility, about the damage, in one month? One year?
   - If the same actions had been directed toward me, how would they have affected me?
   - Would the outcome of my actions have occurred to me, before I had acted on them?
   - What was the extent of the damage?

2. **What is the full measure of *your accountability*?**

   After an evaluation of your actions, it's helpful to consider personal accountability, listing everyone, including yourself, that contributed to your feelings of guilt and shame. Identify what percentage of accountability you see as yours.

3. **Breaking the silence and *making amends (steps five, eight, nine and ten of the twelve-step program)***

Step Five: Breaking Silence

"We admitted to God/higher power, to ourselves, and to another human being the nature of our wrongs."

In this step, you are invited to admit your wrongdoing to yourself, to your higher power, and to another human being. Sit with another person and reveal the nature of your wrongs. As much as you are able, it is important to discuss all details. Don't minimize or exaggerate your wrongdoings. If you cannot remember details, simply make your best effort.

Telling the truth brings a great sense of relief, no matter how unpleasant the details may be. Consider this quote from AA: "You're only as sick as your secrets." Again, it may be frightening to share secrets, but you will feel tremendous relief once you "get it all out." Keeping secrets inside and dwelling on your faults will only allow shame to grow and torment you. A good sponsor, a doctor, therapist, or friend, will never judge or condemn. Admitting faults to another human being is essential to heal. It will free you from guilt and shame, both of which are the results of accumulated wrongdoing.

Step Eight and Nine: Making Amends

Step Eight

"Made a list of all persons we had harmed and became willing to make amends to them all."

Step Nine

"*We made direct amends to such people whenever possible, except when to do so would injure them or others."*

Step eight requires that you make a list of all the people you have harmed and are willing to make amends with. There may be people you think of as unbearable to talk to, which is why it's best to write the list without over-thinking. It's important that you list all of the people you have harmed, whether sexually, physically, or emotionally. You need to "clean up your side of the street." In other words, be willing to do your part, in making amends and leave the results to a higher power. You cannot expect to be forgiven by each person.

Step nine requires you to make amends, whenever possible, directly to those you have harmed, except when this would cause more harm to them. That is why it is vital to have a trusted person or counsellor, with whom to evaluate how each person should be handled. Every situation is different, and, in some circumstances, it is better to avoid direct contact to make amends or avoid sharing all details, out of compassion for that person. If a husband has cheated on his wife, though it's necessary to admit that infidelity, it is not advisable to name names or go into unnecessary detail. Motives should always come from your desire to truly repent for the hurt caused and a genuine wish to offer the best for others. An apology is necessary but not sufficient. You may want to compensate directly to those you have hurt, but this will not be effective without a change of attitude and behavior. If you stole money or lied on expense reports, AA states all those debts must be admitted to and paid back—over time, if necessary.

Sometimes speaking with the person is impossible because of death, distance, or abuse, but while they may not be near you, the negative feelings attached to them are still there. If you want to be at peace with yourself, be willing to be at peace with them. If, for any reason, it is not possible to make amends directly to them, you can write a letter, pray, or use the empty-chair technique. Set up a chair in front of you then express your feeling aloud.

It takes courage and humility to admit wrongs, and there are many barriers that can interfere, with your willingness to make amends directly. Shame is often the cause of inner resistance to apology.

You may also fear a person's anger, worrying that the person you have wronged is upset or furious. Perhaps you have been taught that an apology is a sign of weakness or you might feel residual resentment; believing that the other person was in the wrong and now you expect an apology. You may also think your apology is too late or that it isn't a big deal. The truth is that all those resistances are likely based on your distorted ego perception, which is keeping you from healing your heart.

EXERCISE:

Please make a list of three persons you have harmed in the past. Describe how you harmed them, and how are you going to make amends.

What barriers are interfering with your willingness to make amends directly? Is there a way to overcome them?

Step Ten: Personal Inventory

"Continued to *take personal inventory, and when we were wrong, promptly admitted it"*.

Step Ten suggests that you continue to take personal inventory, as well as admit any new mistakes, as you go forward. A simple way to do this is to pause in the middle of your day, and when you retire at night, take a quick assessment of things. Ask yourself: Was I resentful, selfish or dishonest? Do I owe an apology? Was I kind and loving toward all? What could I have done better? In addition, reflect on the good things that you accomplished and give yourself credit for them. In doing so, try not to exaggerate or dramatize your limitations or your strengths.

4. **Self-forgiveness Letter**

   This involves learning to view yourself with the same kindness and compassion with which you view others. A self-forgiveness letter will help you let go of guilt and shame.

   Write the letter using the following steps:

   - I must forgive myself for these wrongs:
   - My wrongs impacted others and myself in the following ways:
   - Did my life experiences influence my behaviour?
   - Here is what I was able to gather and understand from my experiences:

EXERCISE:

Write a *self- forgiveness letter*

Other Ways to Practice Non-Attachment

Self-Control

Make a list of the habits you want to control and work on. Employ the help of someone close to you or a counsellor, then choose the behavior you'd like to control. Perhaps it is smoking, eating, work habits, alcohol, your temper, shopping, or spending money, etc. When the habit is recognized and acknowledged, set realistic, achievable goals for yourself. Always consider time and avoid dramatic or unsustainable changes. Remember that you're in control of your behavior while making choices.

Generosity and Simplicity

One of the cures for attachment is learning how to practice simplicity in life and giving to others. Simplicity is a state of mind. What matters is not what you have, but how you hold what you have. Spiritually evolved people see possessions and worldly things as irrelevant and temporary; they neither seek nor desire material gain. Instead, they feel more pleasure in sharing with others, and this is especially true for sharing the gift of love and dharma, which means the gift of truth.

See the Impermanence around You and Let Go of Possessiveness

Attachment is reinforced by the denial of the impermanence of worldly things and extends the illusion of possession. To see that all worldly things are transitory can facilitate the letting go of attachment. The inevitable truth is that everything is subject to change and loss. Part of non-attachment is understanding that people and the world around you will change. Not only will you have to allow your life to change, but also yourself. Your children will change, your friends will change, your routines will change, and your living situation might change. As ancient wisdom reminds us, "Ignorance of impermanence generates attachments and therefore suffering, sickness and fear of death." Sometimes your best teacher is death, as it helps you realize that one day, all worldly things will be taken from you and what will remain is the love you have given. For this reason, it is wise to meditate, even on death and on the nature of transitory things.

You may also need to remind yourself that you do not own anything on Earth; everything belongs to the world and goes back to the world. Psychologist Jean Yves Leloup has said, "*. . . to look at an object, a person, or a landscape with love and without attachment, with no desire for appropriation of it, is to see it more clearly . . . we were not created to possess but to be with . . . to think that we can really possess any object or person—even our own bodies, our own thoughts, or our own lives—is an illusion.*"

Meditation, Mantras, and Prayers

Meditation will allow you to practice non-attachment, and you will begin to observe and witness that you are not your body, possessions, thoughts, or emotions. Try to meditate for at least ten minutes, initially, and extend this time daily. When you meditate, take up the position most comfortable for you. Rest and relax. Tell yourself to relax and release all your limbs, as well as your head, neck, and face. While meditating, focus solely on the present moment, letting go of worries about the past or future. Focus on your breathing and, if you feel your thoughts rising, do not interact with them; simply witness your thoughts and let them go. It is in the stillness and silence of the mind/psyche that you may get to know the one who is watching the voice, the true Self. You have the potential within you right now, to experience this peace and joy.

Mantras and prayers are great antidotes for attachment. You may pray to surrender all cravings to your higher power and repeat daily mantras to help release you from possessiveness, attachment/desire.

The following are example of mantras/sentences:

Nothing in this world belongs to me—whether it be an object, person, my own body, thoughts, or knowledge.

I am not my body, nor my thoughts or knowledge, nor my emotions, nor my possessions.

I was not created to possess, but to be with.

I am OK with or without.

Value everything, but become attached to none of it.

Recognize That You Don't Know Everything

Part of being non-attached means recognizing that we don't know everything. We live in a full-dimension movie, where we become deeply absorbed by all experiences, whether physical, mental, or emotional. We can pull back and see that what is perceived is an illusion, a projection of our own level of consciousness.

Ask Yourself, "Who are you?"

If you go to the depth of the question, you will clearly see who you are. Not your name, which is only a collection of letters. Not your body—if you lose your legs, eyes etc., you still exist. You are not your emotions, all of which come and go, whether you are bored, in a good mood, angry, or depressed. Not your thoughts—if you have Alzheimer's, you could lose connection to all thoughts, but you would still exist. You will come to realize that what you truly are is the witness, the observer, the experiencer.

Letting Go of Emotions of Desire

1. **Let go of the Energy of Desire (like dropping a pen)**
    - Be aware of the feeling and feel it in your body
    - Don't condemn or moralize it
    - Just let out the energy behind it
    - Let go of wanting to resist it

- Let go of the fear and guilt that accompanies the process
- Ignore all thoughts and focus on the energy of the feeling
- Thoughts are rationalizations of the mind
- If you get stuck, surrender the feeling of being stuck. Imagine you will receive a ten-million-dollar cheque, if you can let go now.

2. **Sedona Method**

   Allow yourself to feel the feeling then ask, or write, the following:
   - Could I let it go?
   - Would I let it go?
   - When?
   - How do I feel now?

   And keep repeating these questions.

Let Go of Expectations and Attachment to Outcomes

Do your best and expect nothing in return, as it is often your expectations or attachment to outcomes that cause disappointment or other negative feelings. If things don't go as expected, focus only on what you can do in that moment.

Try to let go of your need to control life events and also control the power others have over your happiness.
When circumstances severely upset you, it is an indicator that you are clinging to an expectation, idea, person, or thing. When this happens, try to focus on your breathing. Step away so that you don't react. Return when you feel at peace. If it rains on your wedding day, have your first dance in the rain and find something in the situation that you can enjoy. Clinging to the desire for your wedding to be on a clear, sunny day will only create worry and stress.

Practice the Paradoxical Commandments

The Paradoxical Commandments is an inspirational poem, written by Dr. Kent M. Keith, an American writer and leader within higher education. These guidelines are found detailed, in his book, *Anyway: The Paradoxical Commandments: Finding Personal Meaning in a Crazy World.* Kent's main idea is to encourage people to be kind and loving toward others, by letting go of expectations and attachment to outcomes. The ten paradoxical commandments:

> *People are illogical, unreasonable, and self-centered.*
> *Love them anyway.*
> *If you do good, people will accuse you of selfish ulterior motives.*
> *Do good anyway.*
> *If you are successful, you will win false friends and true enemies.*
> *Succeed anyway.*
> *The good you do today will be forgotten tomorrow.*
> *Do good anyway.*
> *Honesty and frankness make you vulnerable.*
> *Be honest and frank anyway.*
> *The biggest men and women, with the biggest ideas, can be shot down, by the smallest men and women, with the smallest minds.*
> *Think big anyway.*
> *People favor underdogs but follow only top dogs.*
> *Fight for a few underdogs anyway.*
> *What you spend years building may be destroyed overnight.*
> *Build anyway.*
> *People really need help, but may attack you, if you do help them.*
> *Help people anyway.*
> *Give the world the best you have and you'll get kicked in the teeth.*
> *Give the world the best you have anyway.*

Humour in the Moment

Don't take yourself seriously. When you feel the need to cling to someone or to an experience, find humour in the moment. Laughter is the inner child, in you, that sees the world with wonder and joy. If you can laugh heartily, see the absurdity within any situation, where there had been hurt or repulsion, you will release a great amount of tension and stress.

CHAPTER THREE

ACCEPTANCE

The Farmer Story

There is a Taoist story, of an old farmer, who had worked his crops for many years. One day his horse ran away. Upon hearing the news, his neighbors came to visit. "Such bad luck," they said sympathetically. "Maybe," the farmer replied. The next morning the horse returned, bringing with it three other wild horses. "How wonderful," the neighbors exclaimed. "Maybe," replied the old man. The following day, his son tried to ride one of the untamed horses, was thrown, and broke his leg. The neighbors again came to offer their sympathy for what they called his "misfortune." "Maybe," answered the farmer. The day after, military officials came to the village to draft young men into the army. Seeing that the son's leg was broken, they passed him by. The neighbors congratulated the farmer on how well things had turned out. "Maybe," said the farmer.

The story underlines the importance of acceptance and non-attachment, from events beyond our control. When transition happens in our lives, our initial reaction might be to focus solely on the negative aspects. In reality, we don't know what positive changes might also occur. That is the intrinsic nature of change. Over-thinking and analyzing a situation that is beyond our control creates expectations that may not be met, which, in turn, leads to emotional tension.

At a more evolved stage of acceptance, we are able to live with an attitude of surrender to life. Rather than judging the experience unfolding before us, we can simply live in a state of openness to what life brings. When we choose to recognize the positives, we are able to go with the flow of life and see the outcome, good or bad, as manageable. The Chinese proverb that says, "Do not push the river, it flows by itself," is what the ancients called the "Middle Way." In this attitude of acceptance and surrender, we honor the paradox and polarity of life. We can live in the balance point between extremes, by seeing and accepting both sides.

We understand that it is not either/or, wrong/right, good/bad. That is the Middle Way—a way of being in the world. We may not be at this advanced stage of acceptance, but we can practice staying in the Middle Way, through our conflicts, both those within ourselves and with others.

Be like the farmer who hears one opinion and is willing to give thought to the end results, of both sides.

What Is Radical Acceptance?

Radical acceptance is a Buddhist term, also used as a distress tolerance skill, which is part of Dialectical Behavioral Therapy (DBT), developed by Marsha Linehan. It says "yes" to the flow of life, whether pleasant or not, comprehensible or not. Lao Tzu said, "Life is a series of natural and spontaneous changes. Don't resist them; that only creates sorrow. Let reality be reality. Let things flow naturally forward in whatever way they like."

It is normal to experience a temporary fight-or-flight or adrenaline response, when facing an undesirable situation, however the more we grow in acceptance, the faster we let go of any negative emotions associated with it. We can accept rain, on a day planned to visit the beach, by letting go of emotional tension and finding another plan. When we face any challenging situation in life, our ego tends to play the victim. "This is unfair." "Why me?" "Why now?" But it can be liberating to stop playing the victim and focus on what we *can* control. What remains in our control *now* is the replacement of negative emotions, with love and acceptance. Each prevents bitterness, anger, sadness, and unhappiness.

Steps to Practice Radical Acceptance

According to Buddhist philosophy and DBT, there are four steps, to the practice of radical acceptance:

1. ***Notice that you are fighting reality.*** *Be aware of your avoidance of reality.*
2. ***Turn your mind towards acceptance.*** *Utilize your mental power to redirect yourself.*
3. ***Use your body and mind to help you.*** *Choose the most useful technique.*
4. ***Act as if…*** *If you cannot accept anything, act as if you can.*

1. **Notice that you are fighting reality**

First, observe whether you question or dispute reality. To determine your outlook, consider the following questions:

Do you feel bitterness or resentment towards life events or others?

Do you think your life should be different? (It should be like this instead...)

Do you regularly feel unhappy or frustrated with life? Do you think that if something changed, you would be happy? (I'll be happy if I get another job, retire, graduate...)

Do you try to force others to change their behavior?

2. **Turn your mind towards acceptance**

You don't have to go from resistance to acceptance; often, that's too big a leap, but you can make an internal commitment, to stop fighting what *is*. To help turn your mind towards acceptance:

Remind yourself that unpleasant reality is just as it is and cannot be changed (This is what happened.)

Remind yourself that there are "conditions" for the reality outside your control (This is how it happened.)

3. **Use your body and mind to help you**

Practice accepting with your whole self (mind, body, spirit). Use accepting self-talk, relaxation techniques, breathing exercises, mindfulness, or imagery.

It may be useful to use the following imagery techniques:

Imagine sitting in a field watching your thoughts and emotions floating away on clouds.
Picture yourself sitting near a stream, watching your thoughts and emotions drifting past on leaves.

See your thoughts and emotions written in the sand, then watch the waves wash them away.
Visualize your thoughts and emotions passing through one door that opens and closes.

EXERCISE 1:
What is your most common relaxation technique?

Let go of negative self-talk
You can train your mind to focus on anything. If you concentrate on positive self-talk, but have spent years being negative, you'll have to work extra hard to allow yourself time, to overcome a strong belief system. If you frequently dwell on negative self-talk, you will likely experience overwhelming emotions more frequently than most.

EXERCISE 2:

What are your most common negative and positive self-talk thoughts?

"People always hurt me."

"I can't trust anyone."

"I'm unlovable."

"There's something wrong with me."

"I'm broken."

"I'm an idiot."

"I can't do anything right."

"I'm a failure."

"I'm incompetent."

"No one's ever going to love me."

"No one cares about me."

"Everyone always leaves me."

"I'm going to be alone forever."

"I don't deserve to be happy/successful/loved."

Using positive self-talk:

Remind yourself of your strength, your past successes, and your truths.

"Mistakes happen; nobody's perfect."

"This situation won't last forever."

"This situation sucks, but it's only temporary."

"I'm strong and I can deal with this."

"This too shall pass; it might pass like a kidney stone, but it will pass."

"I can be anxious and still deal with the situation."

"I'm strong enough to handle what's happening to me right now."

"This is an opportunity for me to learn how to cope with my fears."

"I've survived other situations like this before, and I'll survive this one too."

"My anxiety won't kill me; it just doesn't feel good right now."

"These are just my feelings, and eventually they'll go away."

"It's okay to feel sad/afraid sometimes."

Use acceptance coping statements:

"I can't change what's already happened."

"It's no use fighting the past."

"Fighting the past only blinds me to my present."

"The present is the only moment I have control over."

"It's a waste of time to fight what has already occurred."

"This moment is exactly as it should be, given what's happened before."

"This moment is the result of a million other decisions."

Make use of the Serenity Prayer
God grant me the serenity to accept the things I cannot change, courage to change the things I can, and wisdom to know the difference.

4. **Act "as if"**

   Even if you're not able to radically accept, try acting "as if."

   If you did radically accept things, what would you do differently? How might you feel?

   List all of the behaviors you would change, if you accepted the facts.

   Rehearse in your mind what you would do, if you accepted what seems unacceptable.

   Allow disappointment, sadness, or grief to arise within you, then let go.

   List pros and cons if you find yourself resisting acceptance.

EXERCISE 3:
What problems or situations should you work on accepting?

Misconceptions of the meaning of acceptance

If I accept what happened,

then I approve of it;

then I like it;

then I'm OK with it;

then I excuse the abuse;

then I absolve of al responsibility the person who deeply hurt me;

then I allow the infidelity;

then I can't do anything about losing my job or losing my home;

then I resign myself to being miserable;

then I keep wallowing and suffering.

Acceptance is not approval

Acceptance does not mean we approve the new reality; rather, acceptance acknowledges it. This means we accept the fact that the reality cannot be changed. Fighting it will only intensify our emotional reaction and create suffering. While pain in life is inevitable, suffering is optional. Suffering is what occurs when we refuse to accept loss or changes in our lives. The process of grieving is often described as having cycles. We usually pass from denial to anger to bargaining, then likely into depression, before eventually turning to acceptance. These stages are not static. Some people move through them in different order, and some do not experience every stage. The final stage of grief is acceptance. If a loved-one passes away and we accept the passing, we focus on coping with the pain of grief. Refusal to accept grief will only create bitterness, anger and resentment. This does not mean we support the loss, but that we accept that the reality cannot be changed.

It is not passivity

Radical acceptance is not passivity. It is the willingness to radically accept reality, as it is and, at the same time, make a commitment to grow and change.

Only when we accept reality can we consider changing it. If we don't like something, we must first accept it the way it is, before trying to change it. Fighting reality with actions such as ranting, judging, and blaming the situation on others, or ourselves, will waste physical and emotional energy. Therefore focus on problem-solving: "OK, this exists. This is happening or happened. How do I want to handle it?"

Remember the three rules: If you have a problem, try to **solve** it or **avoid** it. If you can't avoid or solve it, **accept** it, and even if you *can* solve or avoid it, always keep acceptance in the background.

It isn't suppression or repression

Suppression and repression are defense mechanisms, used as a way to handle feelings. When something is bothering you, you may consciously suppress or unconsciously repress the negative feelings associated with it. Suppression/repression, however, does not make the emotion disappear; it just sits inside, causing more pain. Eventually, the memory associated with this feeling will resurface, and you will unconsciously project it onto others. This way of handling feelings only causes physical, psychological, and social problems. Wise people say that "if you don't like something on the outside, check it from the inside."

Not a one-time thing

Radical acceptance is an ongoing process. In life, we constantly face unpleasant situations, meaning we will constantly have to learn how to accept things. If it is raining on a planned hiking day, we can accept it and move on. There is considerably greater pain, such as the loss of a loved one, or dealing with chronic illness. It is normal to go in and out of acceptance, but after putting years into this practice, we will grow into acceptance more easily. A good way to mature in the path of acceptance is to start with small things. It may be as simple as accepting that driver beeping their horn at us, or another driver cutting us off on the highway.

It is not forgiveness

Acceptance does not mean forgiveness, which extends positive intentions or emotions, towards the offender. Work on acceptance first, then move into forgiveness. Accept reality as it is, without holding negative feelings inside.

It is not liking or disliking reality

Acceptance is not attachment or aversion; rather, it is the Middle Way. Those with great wisdom say that whoever stays in the centre will rise to the top. It is wise to learn how to let go of resistance and attachment, to life experiences, so that we can fully engage in life on its own terms. We can stay centred no matter what happens "out there." No more clinging to, or pushing away reality, because the source of love and happiness arises from within.

The balance between I can, and I cannot; I know, and I don't know

Acceptance requires humility. When we fight against life, we assume to know better. It is worth recalling the farmer story at this point. The truth is that we don't know everything; we experience only .01% of what is going on and miss the other 99.9%. We tend to look at life through tunnel vision. The data we perceive with our senses is limited and statistically insignificant. The real cause of problems is not life, but how our mind perceives life.

We need humility to accept protoplasmic limitations, such as aging, disease, mortality, and genetic predisposition. Michael Singer has said, "Life unfolds based on forces, mostly out of our control." As an embryo inside our mothers, we didn't worry about food, oxygen, and blood supply. Development proceeded as it should, after birth, and as our minds developed we started wanting to control, change, and possess the things around us.

Benefits of Acceptance

Acceptance is increasingly studied for its effectiveness in mental and physical conditions. It was shown to be successful in decreasing stress, anxiety, and depression symptoms as well as in pain reduction.[1-4] Other studies showed the role of mindfulness and acceptance for the severity of psychotic symptoms,[5-6] eating disorders,[7] compulsive sexual behavior,[8] addictive behaviors,[9] suicidal ideation and self-harm,[10] and other mental-health problems.[11]

Acceptance allows one to experience the following:

More emotional stability

Reactions are less intense and shorter in length. We all have mood swings, but the difficulty lies in their intensity and duration, along with our emotional reactions. When in a state of acceptance, there is less fight-or-flight response or sympathetic overstimulation. Therefore, less cortisol secretion and adrenaline release, which are not only the cause of emotional tension but also chronic illnesses.

More freedom and peace, less suffering

People often describe feeling "lighter," "relief," and more at peace. Acceptance is the path of freedom and peace, according to major religions. In Buddhist monasteries, it is advised that if the bell rings while sweeping the floor, stop to learn more about non-attachment and acceptance. It is also by accepting pain that suffering becomes more bearable. Jesus said: "If anyone would come after me, he must deny himself and take up his cross daily and follow me" (Luke 9:23). The cross is symbolic of surrender and acceptance, in the face of pain.

Inner transformation

Acceptance is the key to inner transformation. Psychologist, Carl Rogers, wrote "It wasn't until I accepted myself, just as I was, that I was free to change." The ego can be transcended, only if we accept it with compassionate understanding, not as an enemy to be attacked. We need to first recognize and accept our own limitations in order to change.

"We cannot change anything unless we accept it." ~ Carl Jung.

Life lessons.

Acceptance will help us see negative situations as learning opportunities. Anger stops us from seeing the reality of what is happening and impairs our ability to take the right action and learn from experience. Life is trying to help, by surrounding us with people, places, and things that can stimulate growth.

The world ceases to be a problem

Acceptance means being at peace with what is; knowing that whatever we experience, pleasant or not, it is a product of the creative power of our minds. We alone create our reality perspective, not the situation, another person, or an event. We need to change our state of mind, in order to gradually stop projecting the problem as being "out there."

"Yesterday I was clever, so I wanted to change the world. Today I am wise, so I am changing myself." ~ Rumi

***

CHAPTER FOUR

NON-JUDGMENT

The mind loves to judge; it is a constant judging machine. It fears silence and is addicted to generating "thinkingness." It is basically dualistic and constantly separates mental processing. The duality of the ego/mind is essentially a binary mode of thinking, in which our brain normally operates. Thus, we categorize or divide life into "right/wrong," "good/bad," beautiful/ugly," and so forth. Everything we experience is filtered, categorized, and classified as good, bad, or neutral. When we separate something as "good," we tend to cling to it and grasp for more. When we categorize something as "bad," we hide, resist, and flee from it. With a "neutral" categorization, we choose to ignore it. As a result, our judgmental left-brain creates attraction, revulsion, and indifference. Our life becomes centred on judgments, which create separation.

To categorize things as positive, negative, or neutral is essential to a certain extent. It allows us to make clear decisions and avoid potentially dangerous situations. The issue is that when we over-judge ourselves, others, and the world around us it causes us to perceive life from a reactive and imbalanced mind. It can also cause us to perceive things from the duality of the ego/mind rather than our non-dual Self.

In the process of human evolution, judgment originates from our ego, with all its tendencies to control, project, and dominate. Judgement is our ego's primary defense mechanism, in situations that challenge or threaten us. It is the natural means by which we determine threat and danger—a tool for survival.

Judgement is based on our perception of the world. It is a habit that causes the mind to narrow, so that we see people and circumstances with tunnel vision, based on perception, which is reinforced by previous programming, such as media, family, society, etc.

Judgmentalism is essentially a projection of how we perceive the world, and it reveals what stays repressed within ourselves. What we don't like in others is unconsciously what we have suppressed in ourselves. It is a projection of our interior. Carl Jung wrote, "Projections change the world into the replica of one's own unknown face." Therefore, we need to admit and accept our downside, in order to stop projecting what is wrong/right or condemning others, life, and society. According to Jung, founder of analytical psychology, when we admit the presence of our dark side, including negative thoughts or impulses, we can truly start to be free and let go. We need to be at peace with ourselves in order to be in peace with others. Those who have gained self-knowledge no longer judge others because they have seen their darker side. They stop condemning anyone else and view their mistakes as part of being human. When Jesus said, "Judge not, lest you be judged. For you shall be judged by the judgment with which you judge," the words imply that we enclose the world inside our judgments and perception. The way we judge others is more revealing of ourselves. It shows our personal state of mind and the way we judge others is how we will be judged.

Great spiritual teachers have taught us to go beyond our mind/ego, beyond the psyche, with all its attraction, revulsions, and indifference (i.e., judgments) and identify with our true nature, which is love. Going beyond our judgment doesn't mean becoming indifferent, but simply seeing things as they are. In the Gospel of Judas, when Jesus was asked if his religion was the only true one, He replied, "Every grain of sand may look just like all the others, yet if you look closely, each is different. Think of the water that makes a garden live; the same water makes roses flower red, lilies flower white, and all the other blooms flower in their colors. Is not the beauty of a bouquet due to the harmony and contrast of different flowers? The very differences in our religions and spiritual practices should stimulate us to go farther toward the one God, the unity of all of us. Our differences in languages, races, and cultures are a celebration of the infinite variety of one life.

[...] Only love can empower us to make our differences into a blessing rather than oppositions and exclusions."[1]

This means we should not judge each other according to our differences in religion, beliefs, languages, or cultures, as we are all one through love. We are all from the same source, which is love and love is not something that can be made into an ideology, a power of truth, or a possession. Love is accomplished only through sharing and giving. It does not judge; rather, it connects us and transforms our differences into a blessing and unity. Therefore, seek to understand and forgive rather than condemn. In moving towards love, we may become more discerning of truth, but we have to remember that we still don't know everything.

We cannot entirely comprehend reality. Buddha said that judgment is impossible because perception can see only the limited information and projection of our own psyche (illusion). Perhaps the key is the willingness to admit that our psyche does not know all; thus, we cannot judge, because we do not know the totality of everything. Our judgment is up to life/God/higher power and in realizing that one cannot know everything, we can leave the role of judging to that higher power.

It is rare to find people who live in a near-permanent state of non-judgment. The spiritual journey is one of constant inner transformation; it does not seek perfection but rather transformation and gradual progress. In order to grow, we constantly face difficulties and struggles, including our judgmental left brain. The goal is simply to become aware of our judgments and be willing to let them go, as much as we can. This will reduce emotional disturbances.

Discernment of Truth versus Judgment

When we gain discernment, we are no longer concerned with moralistic judgment, as we intuitively know what works or does not work. We are able to know what is destructive or not, without judging it good or bad. It has been said that when one grows in love and consciousness, one becomes able to see reality, as it is without judgment. Discernment is seeing things through the inner self; judgment sees things through the ego.

What Is Non-Judgment?

The state of non-judgment is the letting go of automatic judgments that arise in our minds with every experience we encounter. Automatic judgments are the result of programming such as media, family, or society, all of which reinforce our likes and dislikes. Non-judgment means experiencing the present moment with neither indifference, attraction, nor revulsion.

We can practice observing things without judging, but we will never be completely free from the processing instrument that is our mind. We cannot control what comes into our minds, as it is in our nature to think. There is an inner dialogue that occurs, that happens independently and spontaneously. We cannot stop the progression of "thinkingness," but we can prevent the course of judgment. Ram Dass writes, "When you go out into the woods, and you look at trees, you see all these different trees. Some of them are bent, and some of them are straight, and some of them are evergreens, and some of them are whatever. You look at the tree, and you allow it. You appreciate it. You see why it is the way it is, you sort of understand that it didn't get enough light, and so it turned that way." Observe things as they are without judgment.

"Thinkingness" is like the movement of ocean waves—it never stops. But in the depth of the ocean, there is a place of pure silence and stillness, like that between two thoughts. A place where there is no judgment. Some sages and saints, while forming different traditions, live in a state of non-judgment. We can practice doing so at any time. In Buddhist tradition, mindfulness and meditation are practiced during a certain time of the day, when one sits still and relaxes while practicing non-judgment. We can think of silence and, if we understand that thoughts come and go, we also can realize it would be impossible to control thought movement. Instead, we need to stop identifying with those thoughts and let them go and let them pass.

Benefits

Countless studies have uncovered the benefits of practicing non-judgement. Studies now show that being less judgmental brings about various positive psychological effects, including increased subjective well-being, reduced psychological symptoms and emotional reactivity, and improved behavioral regulation.[2] Studies have also demonstrated that practicing mindfulness or mindfulness-based therapy (MBT) is a beneficial intervention, to reduce negative psychological states, such as stress, anxiety, and depression.[3-6] Along with that, one may experience more of the following:

Seeing the beauty in everything

When we stop labelling everything as "positive, negative, or neutral," we open ourselves to seeing the beauty in every aspect of life. We stop wanting to control everything with judgment. When busy controlling life, it is always against us. But when we are busy living life, we can best appreciate its beauty.

Increased feelings of gratitude

When we feel what we have is never enough, it generates an endless quest for more. Remaining non-judgmental allows us to feel content, grateful, and satisfied with all we have in the present moment.

Inner peace and joy

Judging ourselves, others, life, and events requires a great amount of energy. An astonishing amount of energy is wasted in living with the need to project judgment onto others. Doing so only contributes to more suffering. The more we grow spiritually, the more we are willing to stop wasting energy judging life. Letting go of judgement and replacing its negativity with acceptance leads to inner peace and joy and frees us from unnecessary emotional pain. This, in turn, will allow us to experience the serenity of the inner self, instead of the continual internal chatter of the mind with its thoughts, emotions, sensations, and memories.

See reality with discernment

Our thoughts create the world that we see. To change the world, we must change our state of mind, allowing reality to come to us, as it is, without judgment. We will see things as they are, including ourselves and others, without adding or subtracting, without projection of memory or influences from earlier conditioning. As we see more clearly, we are more likely to use discernment and see all things with equanimity.

More present with others

It is easy enough to observe that people who judge themselves as well as others will always find problems, whether from the past, present, or in the future. They are lost among their problems. Choosing to avoid such judgment will help prevent viewing life as problematic and will encourage being in the present, with self-possession.

More loving

Living with less judgment frees us, to love and appreciate others as they are. Mother Teresa said, "If you judge people, you have no time to love them," and this is equally true if you live in judgment of yourself.

Develop a Non-Dualistic Mind

Duality compels us to see ourselves as separate from all that surrounds us, but spiritual growth enables us to recognize everything as interconnected, with each encounter and occurrence influencing the next. We discover the limitations of the cause-and-effect model and turn toward a more complex system. What then follows is the result of a broad range of factors: environmental, social, psychological, spiritual, individual, and genetic. From this point, there are conditions that increase or decrease the likelihood of something happening. Observing nature makes this easy to understand. There is infinite functional interconnection and interdependence. Indeed, a garden without care, water, and light will not thrive.

Develop Intuition (right brain)

The right brain controls intuition, creativity, and awareness of the energy around us (e.g., reading people with our hearts rather than our minds).

In true spirituality, there is less judgment, and you can see the bigger picture of life. God sees us with compassion and love. There is a proverb from Shams of Tabriz (Muslim Sufi), "How we see God is a direct reflection of how we see ourselves. If God brings to mind mostly fear and blame, it means there is too much fear and blame welled inside us. If we see God as full of love and compassion, so are we."

Cognitive Distortion

People who tend to be overly judgmental often have irrational ways of thinking (cognitive distortions). Cognitive distortions were developed by psychiatrist Aaron Beck and are part of cognitive behavioral therapy. They are simply ways our mind convinces us that something is false. These inaccurate thoughts are usually used to reinforce negative thinking or emotions. Studying these examples will help to find any that feel familiar to you. Once negative thinking habits can be identified, we are able to distance ourselves from them or replace them with rational thoughts. Negative thoughts tend to occur just before and during distressing situations.

Rationalization

Rationalization occurs when we create excuses for events in life, that don't go our way or for poor choices, made in an attempt to protect us from hurt feelings. We may call them permission-giving statements that give ourselves, or others, permission to do something that can harm our mental health.

Overgeneralization

Overgeneralization categorizes people, places, and events based strictly on personal experience. If a woman has a history of being treated badly by men in the past, she may see all men as cruel. If your first boss was abusive, the experience could lead to you feeling that all employers are abusive. Overgeneralizing risks missing other experiences that don't match a personal stereotype.

Mental Filter (discounting the positive)

Mental filtering rejects positive experiences or creates an inability to see them. Only the bad is noticeable, requiring that anything positive be filtered out.

Critical Self

Self-blame for events outside or beyond personal responsibility.

Mind-Reading

Mind-Reading assumes that you know what others are thinking.

Fortune Telling

The belief that we know what will happen in the future

Jumping to Conclusions

This allows for a negative interpretation despite there being no clear facts.

Compare and despair

This permits only the most positive qualities of others to be seen, while viewing our own in a negative light.

Catastrophizing

The belief that only the worst possible thing will happen.

Black and White (all or nothing) thinking

The tendency to categorize events as black or white, without consideration of anything in between. This views situations in only positive or negative extremes, rather than taking into account that each may, instead, possess both positive and negative aspects.

Magnification

Magnification exaggerates the importance of everything beyond normal proportion.

Personalization

Seeing ourselves as the cause of external negative events.

Labeling

An extreme form of over-generalising. Rather than defining an error, we attach a negative label to ourselves or others: "I'm a loser" or "He's an idiot."

Ways to Practice Non-Judgment

Like any new habit or shift in our mindset, being non-judgmental takes practice. By following these simple steps and becoming aware of and also releasing our judgements, we will be on our way to a more relaxed, open and peaceful mind.

Keep a Journal

Take time during the day to record self-talk in a journal. Reflect on the day's interactions, experiences, feelings, thoughts, and judgments. Try to see if any of them are irrational or negative thoughts. If so, try to replace them with a more rational and positive one. Journaling can help us discover how often we act or react judgmentally and can also assist us with figuring out how to begin to shift this behaviour. It can also offer a greater understanding of, and confidence in, who we are, which could prevent us from comparing ourselves to others.

Meditation

Practicing meditation frees the heart from of all judgement. During meditation, whenever our mind wanders, we practice non-judgment by gently redirecting our attention to the original object of awareness. Meditation grounds us in the moment and helps in moving beyond the conditioning of the mind. It is also useful in detaching from situations and outcomes, allowing us to experience and appreciate things just as they are. Among the most useful meditation apps are: Headspace, Calm, Abide, Insight Timer.

- *Breathing-Meditation Technique: Sitting comfortably and silently, focus your attention on your breath as you let go and relax.*

Place one hand on your abdomen and the other hand on your heart. Breathe in through the nose, for a count of eight and hold for a count of four. Breathe out through the mouth for a count of eight.

Mindfulness-Meditation

Notice when judgments arise. Witness the effect it has on the body and mind, in conjunction with that judgment. Recognize the resulting thoughts without judging or clinging to them. Move forward with clarity, staying present through the experience.

Judgment Diffusion through Visualization

Letting go of Judgment Technique

This requires imagination. People who grow spiritually practice letting go of positive and negative situations. Recall three negative and positive situations.

- *Imagine sitting in a peaceful field, watching your judgments float away on clouds.*
- *Picture sitting beside a stream, as your judgments float past, on beds of leaves.*
- *Envision standing in a room with two doors and seeing your judgments enter through one door and leave through the other.*

Visualization and Guided-Imagery Techniques

Choose a memory of a time that you felt especially good. Close your eyes and imagine it happening again. Who is there, and what are they doing? What colour clothes are they wearing? What sounds do you hear? Breathe deeply and discover the aromas in the air. Relax and enjoy yourself.

- *Take a few slow, deep breaths.*
- *Close your eyes.*
- *Visualize yourself on a beautiful beach, mountain or in a forest.*
- *Imagine yourself smiling, feeling happy, and having a good time.*
- *Make it more vivid in your mind. If you are visualizing the beach, imagine feeling the warmth of the sun on your skin, the smell of the ocean, seaweed, salt spray, and the sound of the waves, wind, and seagulls.*
- *Remain within your scene for five to ten minutes or until you feel relaxed.*

Progressive Muscle Relaxation (PMR)

During this exercise, you will work with almost all the major muscle groups in your body (from forehead to feet), practicing tensing and relaxing muscle groups.

- *Sit or lie down in a comfortable position.*
- *Begin by tensing all the muscles in your face and hold for the count of eight, as you inhale.*
- *Exhale and relax.*
- *Tense your neck and shoulders, again inhaling and counting to eight. Exhale and relax.*
- *Continue down your body, repeating the procedure with the following muscle groups: chest, abdomen, arms, hands (making a fist), buttocks, legs.*

Let Go of First Impressions

Avoid judging others by a first impression. People come in different sizes, shapes, and colors. See that we are perhaps different in appearance, but we are all from the same source, and our differences arise from the development of species, genetics, and conditioning. Let us not judge a book only by its cover.

Avoid Comparisons

Whether comparison leads you to think you're better or worse than someone else, the reasoning in either case is unhealthy. If you must draw comparisons, measure yourself with an earlier version of you. Don't change yourself to simply have people like you. Be yourself, and you'll attract the right people into your life.

Practice Ho'oponopono: Hawaiian Therapy

The releasing method of Ho'oponopono originates from the Hawaiian therapist who cured a hospital ward of criminally insane patients. The treatment involved only the exercising of Ho'oponopono.

The first step asks that you express your regret, for all that has happened. Such an admission may be painful, and you may well resist accepting responsibility for problems "out there."

When you've been able to convey remorse, the second step requires that you ask for forgiveness, not only for yourself but for your ancestors as well.

The third step is the showing of gratitude, for everything that has happened in your life, and the last step shows your love.

In this practice, you see yourself through love. Thus, when one is suffering, we all suffer, as we are all interconnected. When encountering a negative situation, consider saying (in your mind) these four phrases to the person causing the difficulty.

> *I love you, I am sorry, please forgive me, thank you*
>
> *Silently speak each phrase repeatedly when witnessing the negative behaviors of others.*

What if I Must Make a Judgment?

- Seek wisdom and discernment before you speak about sensitive issues.
- Develop an awareness and sensitivity toward others, who have made bad choices.
- Resist the temptation to form quick opinions about people you know (or don't know).
- Have the humility to accept the truth that you do not know everything.
- Desire the best for the person you judge.
- Help others make amends and find self-forgiveness.

EXERCISE:
What benefits would you experience if you start practicing non-judgment?

What cognitive distortion do you usually experience?

What techniques would you use to practice non-judgment?

CHAPTER FIVE

UNCONDITIONAL LOVE

State of Love

Before we discuss unconditional love, let's talk about the word "love." Love takes on different meaning when we speak about God, a partner, a child, a dog, or a country. While the English language uses the same word to describe love, the ancient Greeks used different terms. Their philosophers studied various types of love, which are examined below.

1. **Eros** or **Romanic/Erotic Love**

   I desire your beauty; you give me pleasure.

   Eros is named for the Greek god of love and fertility. As such, Eros is the love of beauty, as a starting point of desire. It is related to sexual appeal, based on the chemistry of a strong physical and emotional attraction. When a relationship is built solely on erotic love, it is said that it "burns hot and bright, but it burns out fast." The physical body and hormones are the main drive for this love.

How to Engage in Eros

Finding sensory pleasure in someone's physical body.

Physical contact, as in hugging and kissing.

Romantic, affectionate connection.

2. **Philia** or **Friendship/Platonic Love**

   I respect you and appreciate your differences, you are my best friend.

Philia is the love between friends, with a shared equality of respect. It's commonly referred to as "brotherly" or "platonic" love," meaning love without sexual interaction. This form of love is often shared amongst those having similar values and interests. Greek philosophers defined it as "affectionate love." They considered philia to be a higher form than Eros. Here, we go beyond the previous stage of love, as another person is not the object of whom we feel dependent on or attached to. We can listen and open up, with trust and less vulnerability. This love is successful as long as mutual respect is understood and maintained.

How to Engage in Philia

Have meaningful conversations with a friend.

Remain approachable, receptive, and trustworthy.

Show compassion and support through difficult times.

3. **Pragma** or **Enduring Love**

   I love you and I want to stay with you for the rest of my life.

   The ancient Greeks defined pragma as "enduring love," which is almost the opposite of Eros (sexual love). While Eros tends to burn out quickly because of its passion and intensity, pragma is a long-lasting love that has matured over time. In this relationship, both partners understand the need to compromise and show equal efforts, to ensure the other person's happiness. Commitment and dedication to making the relationship work are essential to sustain pragma. It is the love of married couples, who have been together for several decades.

How to Engage in Pragma

Ongoing thoughtfulness and awareness, of the need to regenerate the enduring bond.

Show your partner the efforts you're willing to make.

Your primary wish is to live and work with your partner forever.

4. **Storge** or **Familiar Love**

   I am happy, and I become a better version of myself when you are around; I feel affection and tenderness for you.

   Storge is tenderness or familial love. At this stage, love becomes a state of being. We feel tenderness for others and all forms of life. Such love can grow out of friendship (philia), and it illustrates the natural form of affection, experienced between family members, such as parents and their children. It does not consist of physical or sexual attraction, but of a strong bond of familiarity between people. Our memories encourage long-lasting bonds with another individual.

   As we create more memories, the quality of our relationship increases. It is built on acceptance and deep emotional connection. Storge sees the other as a free subject and accepts their alterity. The relationship does not depend on shared equal respect, as in philia. We no longer expect to receive back what we have given. Little by little, we realize that love is fully expressed by "service to others." With the creation of new memories, the value of our relationship increases.

How to Engage in Storge:

Offer time, self, or personal enjoyments, unselfishly to your family.

Let go of resentment toward others, as quickly as possible.

Share memorable moments of personal impact, with family or old friends.

5. **Mania** or **Obsessive Love**

   I love you like crazy; you are mine alone. I cannot live without you.

   Mania is an obsessively passionate love, associated with fear of losing the object of love. It can lead someone into madness, jealousy, possessiveness, co-dependency, or anger.
   The partner becomes part of a survival need.

How to Avoid Mania

Recognize obsessive or possessive behavior, before acting upon it.

Focus more on yourself, than the other person (happiness inside out).

Set boundaries.

Acknowledge and accept inevitable loss.

6. **Ludus** or **Playful Love**

I have fun when you are around.

Ludus is playful, or uncommitted, love. One tends to see love as a game, and it may involve flirting, seducing, and laughter. The focus is on fun, and sometimes, on multiple conquests, without commitment. This love is common in young couples, or at the beginning of a relationship (honeymoon stage), or in uncommitted relationships that some call "friends with benefits." Studies show that when experiencing this type of love, their brains function as if they were taking addictive drugs. Ludus works best when both parties are mature and self-sufficient. "Friends with benefits" problems arise when one party mistakes ludus for eros or storge.

Studies have shown that committed relationships are more beneficial for mental health than uncommitted or casual relationships

How to Exhibit Ludus:

Flirt and engage in humorous conversation with your partner._

Spend time together, laughing and having fun.

Demonstrate ways to show your partner that you trust them and find opportunities to be silly/child-like together.

7. **Philautia** or **Self-love**

I love myself so I can extend this love to others.

The ancient Greek meaning of philautia is the non-narcissistic love we should have for ourselves. Before we can extend love to, or receive it from others, we need to look inward and feel a healthy degree of self-love and consideration. It is the matrix through which we think, feel, act, and relate to others, as well as to the world.

This love involves nurturing and caring for our minds, bodies, and souls. It is much harder to provide for and support others when we are tired and stressed. Conversely, when we feel biologically, psychologically, socially, and spiritually whole and healthy, we are better equipped to care and provide for others. Thus, it is essential to create an environment that fosters our wellbeing. This may include a healthy diet, good sleep hygiene, exercise, breath control, dancing, massage, art, music, being around people, spending time in nature, prayer, meditation, and so on.

How to Show Philautia

Create an environment that nurtures your wellbeing.

Take care of yourself, as a parent would care for a child.

Spend time with people who support you.

8. **Agapē** or **Unconditional Love**

   It's not me who loves, it's the love that loves through me - this love makes the universe move and touches the human soul.

   Agapē is unconditional love, or the highest state of love, and it is rare for humans to reach this level of being. One projects love in all directions, just as the sun shed its light on Earth and creatures, without distinction. It is a universal love that radiates outward, toward all forms of life. At this stage, we are wholly capable of forgiving our enemy. We love unconditionally, with respect for one's freedom. Indeed, to respect freedom means we cannot force anyone to love. When Christ said, "Agapēte allelous" ("Love one another"), He was inviting us to welcome the presence of agapē within us. With unconditional love we still have preferences, but none alter our love toward all beings.

Pure love is often associated with spiritual or divine love. Here we touch on the *Source*, which lacks nothing and gives freely. It is not something we can possess; it is free of attachment and can only expand in sharing (self-fulfilling). It is not something we can lose under certain circumstances; rather, it is constant, permanent, and unchanging. It is neither deserved nor paid for in any way, but simply a gift. An inner decision opens us to agapē**.** We can welcome this gift of love that is within us. The modern concept of such love is altruism, or an all-inclusive love for strangers, nature, animals, victims and criminals, the good and the bad.

It's given without expectation of anything in return.
Some people would describe agapē as a type of spiritual love. Christians believe that Jesus exhibited this kind of love for all humans. He was selfless and sacrificed Himself so that others could be absolved of their sins. He suffered for the happiness of others. Unconditional love is the absolute and ultimate truth, whereas everything else is relative.

The maternal love of a mother for her child is perhaps the best way to illustrate this love. Imagine a mother visiting her son, a murderer, in prison. She does not condone his actions but loves him unconditionally and forgives him, despite them.

Romantic vs Agapē

Romantic love is often confused with unconditional love. Let's examine these differences.

Romantic love

Is based on attraction and fades, after the objective is realized.

Transient: You can gain it or lose it, and this can cause fear and/or anticipation of loss.

Stimulated by adrenaline and sex hormones.

May cause impaired judgment, attachment, possessiveness, and control.

Anticipation of loss can cause rage, jealousy, even suicide or murder.

Continues for years, only when combined with other types of love.

Unconditional love:

Sees the essence, beauty, and love in everything.

Permanent, continuous, and self-fulfilling.

Starts as a personal decision then emanates from the heart.

Increased discernment of truth, non-attached, non-possessive.

Release of endorphins.

Benefits of Unconditional Love (Healing Love)

To advance toward unconditional love is the goal of major religions and spiritually committed people. Well-intentioned human beings, who want to improve the world, will succeed to a certain point and, ultimately, fail if they ignore the underlying cause: lack of love. We can heal the world through love, as it is a healing energy. It restores the absence of love, which causes isolation and suffering. Love's energy is all-encompassing and transforms the world around us. This phenomenon is called the non-verbal effect of the energy of love. We change the world not by what we have or do, but by what we have become. This love is a state of being, meaning it springs from the heart, not from the mind, enabling our presence to touch human souls.

Perhaps you remember a time with someone that radiated such love and felt your heart uplifted, by the presence of love.

Psychiatrist David Hawkins, in his book, *Letting Go: The Pathway of Surrender*, tells the story of a hunter who shot a flying duck. The bird fell to the ground badly injured. The female mate flew down and spread her wings over the injured duck, to shelter him. When the hunter witnessed this act of love, his heart changed, and he vowed never to hunt again. Experiencing unconditional love can transform our lives.

Some believe that unconditional love is the ultimate law of the universe. That love is the ultimate truth, and everything else remains relative. When one loves at this level, a critical discernment of truth and wisdom has been gained. This way of being supports life, in a natural sense, achieving a profound understanding of the truth of life, in all natural forms. One knows in their heart what truth is.

When we love, we seek to understand ourselves and others and the errors they have made. Understanding leads to forgiveness. Thus, unconditional love leads to unconditional forgiveness, and with forgiveness, we are able to let go of negative feelings such as guilt, shame, and bitterness. With lovingness and forgiveness, letting go becomes more instinctive, continuous and effectively healing.

Additionally, love empowers us to do things we never thought were possible. It helps potentiality become actuality, when other conditions are present. This energy becomes a catalyst and this love can be seen in support groups, where love and acceptance, among members, are a motivation for change.

Love enables us to feel more connected to others and the world around us; we feel our oneness with all of life, because we can see love, as the essence of all things. It helps us go beyond, and can dissolve, the ego. Therefore, beyond the duality of the mind, there is no separation, only oneness. Research studies suggest that loving-kindness meditation (LKM) and compassion meditation (CM) are highly promising practices, for improving positive feelings and reducing stress and negative emotions, like anxiety and mood symptoms. LKM aims to develop an effective state of unconditional kindness, to all people, whereas CM involves techniques to cultivate compassion, or deep, genuine sympathy for those stricken by misfortune, together with an earnest wish to ease their suffering. LKM and CM have been described as paths toward a profoundly spiritual transformation that may help cultivate an appreciation for our oneness and an awareness, of the suffering caused by separation as well as the happiness of knowing our connection with all beings.(1)

Recent studies have shown that the brain of those experiencing unconditional love changes neurologically. It alters the chemistry of our brains physiology. The neuronal connections change due to a shift in the brain's energy balance.[2-3] Lovingness changes brain physiology from left brain (reason) dominance, to right brain (intuitive).

Lovingness has a powerful effect on a person's happiness, and it reduces emotional disturbances. Research demonstrates that love activates the release of neurotransmitters and hormones (serotonin, dopamine, oxytocin, and endorphins) related to feelings of wellbeing and it reduces anxiety and stress. [4]

Psychologist Abraham Maslow supported the idea that individuals need unconditional love in order to grow. Additionally, Holocaust survivor and psychiatrist, Dr. Viktor Frankl, writes, in his book, *Man's Search for Meaning:*

> *Love unconditionally is essential for living a meaningful life.*
>
> *Love is the only way to grasp another human being, in the innermost core of his personality.*
>
> *No one can become fully aware of the essence of another human, being unless he loves him.*
>
> *By love, the loving person enables the beloved person to actualize their potentialities.*

According to quantum physics, the law of attraction, self-fulfilling prophecy, and from my clinical experience, I see that what is held in the mind, i.e., feelings, thoughts, and intentions, is inclined to manifest. If we hold on to negative feelings such as anger, resentment, hate, or jealousy, we will find ourselves surrounded by angry people. If we remain filled with fear, we are more likely to be surrounded by fear-provoking events.

On the other hand, if we are full of love and compassion, we will attract more loving people. Therefore, we need to change our thoughts and feelings about others if we want others to change their feeling about us. For others to become more loving toward us, we first need to love them. Ultimately, love will change us and those around us.

Tips on Moving Towards Agapē

There are barriers in moving towards unconditional love: an unpleasant past, genetic factors, social programming, and belief systems, however, as mentioned earlier, it is an inner decision to move toward lovingness. With dedication and willingness it's a possible goal for everyone to achieve. Traditional wisdom encourages us to do so. Jesus said, "Love your enemy." Buddha taught that "hate is not conquered by hate; hate is conquered by love." Let's consider some useful tips for moving towards agapē.

Love yourself unconditionally first.
And God said, 'Love your enemy,' and I obeyed him and loved myself. ~ Kahlil Gibran

Unconditional love starts at home, with oneself. We must love ourselves, before we can extend love to others. We know our limitations and shortcomings better than anyone. Therefore, if we can love ourselves, despite the awareness of our own limitations, we will be able to offer the same to others. There is a well known quote, from the late American poet and civil rights activist, Maya Angelou, that says "Do the best you can until you know better. Then when you know better, do better."

We must accept and forgive ourselves, for not being perfect and for things we did at times, when we did not have enough knowledge or experience. If we never see ourselves worthy of unconditional love, we will never be able to see ourselves worthy of offering it. You can't pour from an empty cup.

Choose to forgive yourself and others for everything and seek to understand (forgiveness letter).

The key to moving towards unconditional love is the willingness to forgive ourselves and others, for everything. This will allow us to let go of negative feelings and bring about healing. With such forgiveness, we can let go of guilt, shame, bitterness, anger, and resentment. Now ask yourself, what havent I forgiven in myself or others?

Unconditional forgiveness is not something that our ego/mind is capable of; it emanates from the heart. It is not something we think about, but something we become; essentially, a state of being. It means trying to forgive everything, whatever it may be, including those that never apologize to us and even our enemies. We love them as human beings, subject to human limitations. We strive to feel compassion toward their ignorance without condoning their behaviours. Their actions may stem from not knowing any better, from lack of love or discernment of truth in their lives. In religious term, it translates to "hate the sin, love the sinner." Loving someone unconditionally does not compel us to approve of their behavior, but to "forgive them, because they know not what they do," as Jesus said.

I would say that the only sin is to lack love. In other words, agapē is the absolute truth, and everything else is relative. It is also said that what we forgive in others will be forgiven in ourselves. That which we forgive in others is grounded in our own perceptions. Deeply spiritual people believe there is nothing to forgive, since everything is already forgiven. Again, to forgive from the heart can take time, and it's an ongoing process. Still, if we dedicate ourselves to love, we will better understand others, as love brings compassion and the desire to understand, rather than condemn, and with understanding one can forgive.

When we face injustice, there is something within us, unwilling to forgive. We look for justice and may feel bitter, in the face of inhuman behaviors, but forgiveness should have the last word. We need to try and let go of negative feelings, in order to feel whole, as forgiveness does not enclose individuals within the negative consequences of their actions. Existing suffering does not need to be complicated, by adding more suffering in our lives, as this will inevitably reflect chaos. Forgiveness permits us to let go and allow life to be the force, in control of justice. In doing so, we activate more joy and peace. To heal our hearts, we need to forgive past wounds and realize that the process of life controls the path to justice, and we do not. This reasoning will remove a significant amount of stress from our lives. We all reap what we sow; all thoughts and actions have consequences and, one day, we will have to bear those consequences.

With forgiveness, we also need to set boundaries. Forgiveness doesn't mean letting others take advantage of us. It's sometimes best to remove ourselves from an environment in which we are repeatedly mistreated, as this can be a loving choice for both parties. Under such circumstances, it is helpful to avoid the negative and, at the same time, be forgiving towards others, displaying your best intentions.

Choose to see beauty in all life instead of the imperfection

To love unconditionally is to see the beauty, perfection, and constant presence of love, everywhere. Like the sun, we can shine equally on all living things, radiating love everywhere, instead of projecting judgment onto the world.

Let go of attachment and possessiveness

Love is all-inclusive and knows how to share, rather than remaining attached to what it possesses, whether it be knowledge or a material possession. Agapē offers more joy in giving and sharing and is not prideful about possessions. Nor does it expect anything in return. Expectation leads only to more attachment, putting pressure on others and causing inner resistance and defensiveness. Love is a primary energy, and everything else is secondary.

To embrace unconditional love, we must embrace non-attachment, as discussed in the first chapter. Practice non-attachment toward money, homes, cars, expectations, plans, outcomes, and the like.

Accept oneself, others, and all life experience

If we want to move toward lovingness, we need to accept life experience, as much as we can. This means breaking away from the desire to control or make changes to everything. Loving unconditionally helps us see perfection, in all things and accept what comes to us, via others and the world as it is. We can choose to view negative experiences as an opportunity to grow.

God grant me the serenity to accept the things I cannot change, courage to change the things I can, and wisdom to know the difference. ~ Reinhold Niebuhr

Choose love without expecting anything in return

Dedicate your life to improving the lives of others with love, without expecting anything in return. You may offer your time, charity, money or advice, to someone in need. What might be a loving act towards one person could be different for another. If you have two friends dealing with the loss of a loved one, being the shoulder to cry on and engaging in long talks may be the loving choice for one, while just being present and silence may be what's needed for the other. Ask yourself: "How can I help with this right now?

Be willing to practice unconditional love towards all forms of life

Unconditional love is not limited to human beings and includes all of life. Have the willingness to *love yourself, others, and all forms of life, all the time, everywhere, under all conditions, without exception.*

Ask yourself: Are you expressing unconditional love towards all of life and its experiences?

Try to do this at least once a day. Show your love to Mother Nature, be loving to a pet, give something, without any expectations in return, tell someone you love them, without expecting to hear it back, let someone into your lane during rush hour and open the door for someone.

Be willing to replace fear with love

The antidote for fear is love. Sages and saints, from all religions, have said that love casts out fear. In the state of agapē, there is nothing to fear, because there is nothing to lose. Agapē is unchanging, permanent and always within. It is not something we can lose. If our love or happiness comes from an exterior source, we will feel a fear of loss, however if that love comes from within, it wont be dependent on outside circumstances. Instead of fearing the loss of another, we may want to appreciate the present moment, by loving them. Fear of job loss may be replaced by showing love to our fellow workers. Fear of weight gain may be replaced by loving our bodies.

Engage in support group meetings such as AA, SMART recovery or refuge recovery groups

These groups encourage us to move upward, towards lovingness and are great examples of where you can experience a high form of love. These groups love you, not for what you do or what you have but for what you are—a fellow human.

Practice the Five Love Languages

Ancient Greeks weren't the only ones to study love. Over a long period of time, relationship therapist, Dr. Gary Chapman, identified five languages of love, through his work with couples. His book, *The Five Love Languages: How to Express Heartfelt Commitment to Your Mate*, provides a lot more detail.

In a nutshell, Chapman argues that each of us gives and receives love differently, but all fall into five categories:

1. **Words of Affirmation**

   Some people want to hear "I love you," or other positive words, from their partner. Without them, they feel unloved.

2. **Acts of Service**

   Doing nice things for your partner is an act of service, whether it be changing the oil in the car, cleaning the house, making dinner or doing things to help make the other person happy.

3. **Receiving Gifts**

   Some people value giving and receiving gifts, and some do not. If you measure your partner's love by how many gifts you are given, your love language is "receiving gifts."

4. **Quality Time**

Other people measure the quality of their love by how much time their significant other wants to spend with them. Without enough "together time," they can feel unloved.

5. **Physical Touch**

   Some individuals associate love with physical touch, from handholding to cuddling to sex, counts as "physical touch."

Attachment Theory and Love

Past experiences, especially from childhood, can affect how much we're able to share love with another. Secure relationships, with our parents, make it easier to offer love as an adult, but insecure, unhealthy relationships, with our early caregivers, can leave us uneasy about it.

Attachment theory can teach us how these dynamics work and is the psychological principle concerning relationships, between humans. The important point of this model is that young children need to develop a relationship with at least one primary caregiver, for normal social and emotional development. It was developed by psychiatrist and psychoanalyst, John Bowlby, and was extended to adult romantic relationships, in the late 1980s, by Cindy Hazan and Phillip Shaver.

There are four major attachment styles, that are formed in early life, and which people are likely to have later in adult life. These styles explain how we relate to others, based on our personality traits.

There are four adult attachment styles:

1. ***Secure***
2. ***Anxious-Preoccupied***
3. ***Dismissive-Avoidant***
4. ***Fearful-Avoidant***

Secure Attachment Style

Those with a strong, secure attachment style regularly manifest some of the following traits:

Higher emotional intelligence (effective communicators).

Appropriate and constructive communication of emotions.

Sound ability to send and receive healthy expressions of intimacy.

Knows when to draw healthy, appropriate, and reasonable boundaries.

Feels confident whether alone or with a companion.

Inclined towards having a positive view of relationships.

Likelier to take interpersonal difficulties in stride.

Prefers to solve problems through discussion, rather than with an antagonistic attitude (excellent conflict resolution).

Resilient in the face of relationship dissolution.

Has a willingness to grieve, learn, and move forward.

For these people, unconditional love is practiced with ease.

People that have a secure attachment style are not perfect. They too can experience highs and lows, just like everyone else, but their mature approach to relationships reflects the healthiest of the four adult attachment styles.

Anxious-Preoccupied Attachment Style

Those with the anxious-preoccupied attachment style consistently demonstrate several of the following traits:

Nervousness and insecurity in relationships.

Relationship stressors, based on real and imagined actions and events.

Tendency towards neediness, possessiveness, jealousy, control, oversensitivity, and obsessiveness.

Propensity for negative reasoning (a partner socializing with friends leads the other partner to think, "He doesn't really love me. I was right not to trust him." Actions are then taken, that inevitably pushes the partner away).

Requires constant validation to feel secure and accepted.

Leans towards desperation, to form a fantasy bond (wanting someone loving at all times).

Feels an emotional hunger for love.

Looks to a partner to feel rescued or complete, for a sense of safety and security.

Drama-oriented personality.

Constantly struggles with relationship issues, in order to attain validation, reassurance, and acceptance.

For some, they feel more comfortable within stormy relationships.

Uneasiness when alone.

Seeks high levels of intimacy, approval, and responsiveness from partners.

Less trusting.

Preserves negative views about themselves and their partners.

High levels of emotional expression.

Overreaction to expected separation or actual separation.

Painful cycle of self-fulfilling prophecies and self-sabotage.

Frequently seeks a dismissive-avoidant partner.

Dismissive-Avoidant Attachment Style

This style is observable through several of the following traits, shown on a regular basis:

Extremely self-directed and self-sufficient.

Desires a high level of independence (behaviorally and emotionally).

Viewing oneself as not needing close relationships.

Avoidance of true intimacy, believed to make one vulnerable (emotional obligations).

Pushing away those that get too close ("I need room to breathe.")

Other priorities in life are found to be more important than romantic relationships (work, social life, personal projects, and passions, travel, fun, etc.)

Frequently excluding the partner.

Commitment issues. Some prefer to be single.

Has few, truly close, relationships.

Seeks isolation and feeling "pseudo-independent."

Passive-aggressiveness and/or narcissism.

Tendency to suppress emotions.

Deals with conflict by distancing themselves from their partner.

Lacks interest in forming close relationships.

Feels considerable distrust in others.

Creates high levels of self-esteem by investing in personal abilities or accomplishments.

Maintains a positive view of self, based on personal achievements.

Explicit rejection or minimizing the importance of emotional attachment

Indifference towards the opinions of others.

Low psychological intimacy (one-night stands, sex without love).

Feels vulnerable when faced with a crisis.

Fearful-Avoidant Attachment Style

Those that have this style repeatedly exhibit several of the following emotions and traits:

Grief, PTSD, neglect, abandonment, and abuse after especially challenging life experiences.

Mixed feelings about close relationships (desiring them and, simultaneously, feeling uncomfortable with emotional closeness).

Desiring but concurrently resisting intimacy.

Struggles with feeling confident towards others and relying on them.

As with the Anxious-Preoccupied Style, they are suspicious of others' intentions, words, and actions.

As with the Dismissive-Avoidant Style, they push people away.

Mistrust towards partner and views self as unworthy.

Like dismissive-avoidant people, fearful-avoidant adults often seek less intimacy, suppressing their feelings.

Fear of being too close to or too distant from others.

Overwhelmed by emotional reactions and often experiences emotional storms.

Likely to be mixed up or unpredictable in their moods.

They have the belief that they must cling to others to get their needs met, but in doing so, someone will likely get hurt.

The person they want to go to for safety is the one they fear being close to the most.

They find themselves in rocky or dramatic relationships, experiencing many highs and lows.

Ongoing fear of abandonment and coexistent struggle with intimacy.

Final thoughts:

Insecure individuals, more often than not, attract those equally insecure, and secure individuals attract secure individuals. Insecure relationships are less emotionally satisfying than secure attachments, as those less secure cannot practice unconditional love. Secure individuals cope with loss more easily (death, rejection, infidelity, abandonment, etc.).

Attachment styles are both genetic and environmental. They are developed in childhood and are passed down, through our genetics. Children learn how to connect, relationally, from their parents and caregivers, and what they learn they apply to their adult relationships. Our attachment history plays a crucial role in determining how we relate in adult romantic relationships, and how we connect to our children. When our caregivers reject us or are unresponsive to our needs, we may develop an insecure-avoidant or dismissive-avoidant attachment style. Children who experience persistent neglect or abuse may develop a fearful-avoidant or disorganized-disoriented attachment style. They may fear both intimacy and being alone. If caretakers fluctuate between being responsive to our needs or being dismissive and neglectful of them, we may develop an insecure-ambivalent or anxious-preoccupied attachment style. Thus, any negative experience with caregivers can cause negative attachment styles that will lack the ability to provide unconditional love, within relationships.

***

CHAPTER SIX

POWERLESSNESS

Powerlessness is often mistaken for weakness, but it is more an attribute of strength, because it requires genuine humility and honesty. Admitting powerlessness means learning to surrender, that which cannot be controlled. This admission can be difficult for the ego/ human psyche, however the ego's surrender, of its illusion of control, is the foundation of recovery. It is by humbly admitting our limitations that we can open ourselves up, to receiving help from others and from a power greater than ourselves.

Powerlessness and the act of surrender are critical steps in Alcoholics Anonymous and other twelve-step programs. The twelve steps are a valuable resource, for someone in recovery from alcohol and drug addiction, and it is worth considering that these steps have a more general use also. They can be applied to whatever life problems we have or be used in an effort to grow spiritually. These steps are simply a spiritual way of living in the world. The first three steps illustrate the idea of powerlessness.

What Are the Twelve Steps?

The twelve-step program is a set of guiding principles and a course of action, for recovery, from all forms of addiction and psychological problems. Originally proposed by Alcoholics Anonymous (AA), as a method of recovery from alcoholism, the program was first published in 1939. *Alcoholics Anonymous: The Story of How More Than One Hundred Men Have Recovered from Alcoholism* was generally known as *The Big Book.* The method was then adapted and became the foundation of other twelve-step programs. The fellowship of AA, or twelve-step programs, is based upon reconnecting and making peace with oneself, others, and one's higher power. The underlying principle of the program is that we are healed by sharing our experiences with each other, in love and honesty. "Together, we can do what none of us could accomplish alone."[1-2]

The Twelve Steps

1. *We admitted we were powerless over our problems (addictions, chronic pain, relationships, etc.) to the point where our lives had become unmanageable.*
2. *Came to believe that a power greater than ourselves could restore us to sanity.*
3. *Made a decision to turn our will and our lives over to the care of God/Higher Power.*
4. *Made a searching and fearless moral inventory of ourselves.*
5. *Admitted to God/Higher Power, to ourselves, and to another human being the exact nature of our wrongs.*
6. *Ready to have God/Higher Power remove all these defects of character.*
7. *Humbly asked Him to remove our shortcomings.*
8. *Made a list of all persons we had harmed and were willing to make amends to them all.*
9. *Made amends directly to these people wherever possible, except when to do so would injure them or others.*
10. *Continued to take personal inventory and, when wrong, promptly admitted it.*
11. *Sought through prayer and meditation to improve conscious contact with God/Higher Power, as we understood Him/Her, praying only for knowledge of the Divine Will for us and the power to carry that out.*

12. *Having had a spiritual awakening as the result of these steps, we try to carry this message and practice these principles in all our affairs.*

Twelve-Step Summary

Admitting that one cannot control one's addictions.

Recognizing that a higher power can provide strength, while *examining past errors, with the help of a sponsor.*

Making amends for these errors.

Helping others who suffer from the same addictions.

In this chapter, we will focus only on the first three steps and explore the meaning of powerlessness.

Step One

"*You admit that you are powerless over your problems (e.g, addiction) and that your life has become unmanageable.*"

The first step occurs when you become aware, that you are powerless over the problem that is making your life unmanageable. Taking this step breaks through denial, and you are then able to be honest about your condition. You acknowledge the limitations of the ego, and that you have no sense of being able to solve this problem, alone, through your own efforts. Admitting your life is unmanageable means that you don't have control, over unfolding, daily events. It is a clear acceptance of your condition.

There are, of course, things in life you can change and control, however when they become addiction and mental-health problems, you may feel that there are too many things you cannot control.
As mentioned before, this first step usually refers to alcohol or drug addiction, but it can relate to any addiction or life problem(s) you have. In the case of alcohol or drug addiction, powerlessness is the inability to say no to the first drink or drug. It is the compulsion to keep using the addictive substance, despite severe consequences, whether it be

financial, social, legal, etc., making life unmanageable. The first part, "powerlessness," defines the problem as: the inability to resist the first use. The second part, "our lives have become unmanageable," deals with the inability to control ourselves, after the first use. It describes the effect that the problem has had on our life.

Step Two:

Came to believe that a power greater than ourselves could restore us to sanity.

The moment we accept our powerlessness, we are then ready to move to Step Two. This step is the recognition that a power, other than our own ego, is capable of restoring us to sanity. Once we lose the ability to regulate drug use, *The Big Book* says, "probably no human power" can revive it. The solution here is to find a higher power greater than ourselves.

Perhaps you object to the idea of a higher power or have reservations about accepting *any* concept, of a power greater than yourself. If this is how you feel, a helpful objective is to try and find ways to break through anger or doubts and keep an open mind. The atheist or agnostic, who wants nothing to do with God, can still make a start on Step Two. It is suggested in AA to "fake it till you make it." Follow your sponsor's advice to give prayer a chance. Experience shows that those that force themselves to pray on a daily basis see growth in their spiritual life, even if slowly. All one needs is to be open to spiritual principles. The step doesn't say "we believe in a higher power;" it says "we *came* to believe." It is a process.

Step Three

Made a decision to turn our will and our lives over to the care of God as we understood Him/Her.

Step Three is the point where you willingly decide to surrender your ego to God, as you understand Him/Her. More precisely, it is the decision to surrender your thoughts, will, actions, problems, and your life over to the care of a higher power. The essence of Step Three is the decision to rely on the guidance of a higher power, rather than relying on an inflated sense of ego or willpower. In *The Big Book*, a prayer is suggested for this step of surrendering: "God/Higher Power, I offer myself to you, to build with me and to do with me as you will. Relieve me of the bondage of self, that I may better do your will. Take away my difficulties, that victory over them may bear witness to those I would help of your power, your love, and your way of life. May I do your will always!"

Making a decision to turn to the care of a higher power needs dedication. Simply deciding, without following up with action, is meaningless. While you work on what you are able to in your life, seek guidance from your higher power, without worrying about the result. The Serenity Prayer can help, as you seek knowledge and make the decision to turn your will over to God: "God, grant me serenity to accept the things I cannot change, courage to change the things I can, and wisdom to know the difference."

How do we know the difference between the voice of ego and the voice of intuition/God?

A common answer, from AA members, is that the voice of ego is impatient, prideful, and self-centered, whereas the voice of the Self/God/Higher Power brings peace, kindness, love, and compassion. They also say that "higher power speaks to us through people." Therefore, listen to feedback and keep praying for higher-power guidance. It is also helpful to talk with your sponsor, counsellor, doctor, or therapist on a regular basis and use the opportunity to discuss your life decisions.

What is "God as we understand Him/Her"?

Everyone has thoughts and ideas about God or a higher power. You may consider a power greater than yourself as God, Creator, nature, true self, energy, pure consciousness, higher intelligence, or a greater force. In the end, the names don't matter. What really matters is that you believe you are not the creator nor the center of the universe, and you cannot control everything. The world belongs to God, evolution, creation, and cause and effect, but it doesn't belong to you.

Why do some people resent the word "God"?

There are many distortions, misinterpretations, and misconceptions regarding God, which only creates further separation and suffering. Perhaps you have an image of a God, who is vengeful, judgmental, and punitive. You may resent God, in the belief that religious worship encourages judgment toward others, intolerance, hatred, and war. You might say that religions have created corruption and trauma (physically and sexually abused children), resisted the advancement of modern science, and have discouraged people from living their fullest life on Earth. I believe, however, that the more we understand the nature of love, the more we know the nature of God, which is different from the image of God, projected by others. People rebel more against their own image of God, rather than the idea of God. Behind any religion or tradition, we will always find those who are more devoted to spiritual truth and integrity. This applies to anything in life—we may find rude doctors, or careless drivers, but neither define the standard for all. An old adage fits well here: "Don't throw the baby out with the bathwater." The bathwater may be dirty, but why throw out the baby, in frustrated haste, to solve the problem?

Is belief in a higher power good or bad?

Studies suggest that the benefit of spiritual involvement depends on one's perception of God.[3] Having a positive image of God as powerful, loving, caring, and merciful, is related to better mental health and wellbeing.[4] On the other hand, belief in a powerful, angry, punishing, and unforgiving God creates fear, guilt, and anger that may worsen mental health.[5-6] Not believing in God at all may be better than believing in an angry and punitive God,[7] whereas belief in a distant, unavailable God, or having a lack of personal connection, is not likely to influence mental health anymore than not believing in God.[8] The spiritual journey through the twelve steps can be successful, only if one understands the true nature of God, which is love.

Do the twelve steps and the idea of powerlessness/spiritual awakening help recovery?

Alcoholics Anonymous, and other twelve-step programs, offer a method of recovery, which is known to be more effective, than psychotherapy, in achieving abstinence, according to a recent comprehensive analysis, published in the Cochrane Library. This review found that 42% of AA participants were completely abstinent one year later, compared with 35% of participants who underwent other treatments, like Cognitive Behavioral Therapy (CBT).[(9)]

EXERCISE:

Describe your understanding of your higher power.

Explain what a spiritual experience is to you. How do you think it differs from an emotional or physical experience?

What does surrender mean to you? What feelings do you have, with respect to the word?

Which part of your life are you most willing to turn over to a higher power?

List recent examples of turning your will over to your higher power and acting in faith.

When you sense there is something you need to be doing, how do you determine whether your higher power or your ego is talking to you?

What are you thankful for? What are you sorry for? What are you angry about with your higher power? What do you need from your higher power?

EXERCISE:

1. *How has addictive behavior endangered your life or the lives of others?*

2. *What does loss of control and unmanageability look like to you?*

3. *List times when you started out "in control," but then "lost control," by drinking or drugging, more than you had intended. How did you suffer the consequences?*

4. *List three feelings you have tried to alter, through the use of mood-altering drugs.*

5. *Give three reasons why you would want to stop using alcohol/drugs.*

CHAPTER SEVEN

GRATITUDE

There are many reasons, we can find, to be grateful, for what's been given to us. If we observe nature carefully, we see trees, birds, plants, animals, and rivers. We may ask why such great beauty surrounds us. Perhaps it's a gift to us from life, just as our life is a gift. There are those who are never grateful for what they have, and others who are happy with a ray of sunshine or a smile. We can all learn moment-to-moment gratitude, however we must first realize the precious gift of life, in all forms, including our own.

What Is Gratitude?

Derived from the Latin word "gratia," gratitude means gratefulness or thankfulness. It refers to a "state of thankfulness" or a "state of being grateful." Harvard Medical School defines gratitude as "a thankful appreciation for what an individual receives, whether tangible or intangible. With gratitude, people acknowledge the goodness in their lives. As a result, gratitude also helps them connect to something larger than themselves as individuals–whether to other people, nature, or a higher power." As we grow spiritually, gratitude becomes a state of mind, independent of conditions. We are able to honor all life experiences, agreeable or not, comprehensible or not. Unconditional gratitude is the high road. We are no longer caught in the melodrama of life and can live gratefully, even in the midst of chaos. We may rarely see people at this stage, but we can develop this sense of gratitude, which will lift our hearts upward, toward peace and inner joy.

Benefits

More connected with all forms of life and a higher power.

In gratitude, we can feel reverence, for the beauty of all creation and the Source of life. We not only see the beauty in all of life, but we recognize its sacredness and treat it with respect. When we reach full realization, we may walk more carefully on Earth. For example, we see each meal as an offering gift, a sacrifice from another form of life, and we feel grateful for that gift. We see that the world around us is interconnected, interdependent and we feel peace within ourselves, if all of life is treated with love and respect. The world is not a place for exploitation and simply fitting in, but one of communion and love. A Vietnamese proverb teaches that when eating fruit, remember the one who planted the tree. This reminder cultivates a sense of thankfulness for our ancestors and the earth, which provides all we need to sustain life. A mind full of gratitude will not only help to cultivate a sense of wonder for all creation; it will also increase feelings of connectedness with nature, others, and the Source of life.

More positive emotions such as inner peace and joy

Gratitude for all of life's experiences is ultimately the key, to long-lasting joy and peace. We cannot control all of life's happenings; sometimes they can be agreeable, and other times not, but we can change the way we view them. We each endure struggles of many kind, whether it be an illness, the loss of a loved one, or the ravages of war etc. Buddha said that life is suffering; it is part of our journey. What best defines the experience is our perception of circumstances. If we practice unconditional gratitude, we start observing life experience with mindfulness, non-judgment, and acceptance. During a lecture, Thich Nhat Hanh stated, "With all I have experienced in my life, the power of gratitude stands above everything else. In your mindfulness practice, use gratitude until it becomes your way of life. Once you develop more of this habit, you will truly feel more positive energy surrounding yourself no matter the situation. You will be able to say to yourself, 'although I wouldn't want to live through it again, I am grateful for that experience."

With a negative experience, remember that all struggles are temporary, and try to see it as a learning opportunity. Carl Jung said: "Be grateful for your difficulties and challenges, for they hold blessings; they are necessary for healthy personal growth, individuation, and self-actualisation." You can also choose to see the struggle as a way to prevent a bigger problem. Jung further stated: "The word happiness would lose its meaning if it were not balanced and contrasted and compared to sadness. In comparing how an experience could have been worse we develop gratitude and happiness, while if we compare it with how it could have been better, we develop bitterness and sadness." Therefore, we can view any struggle as an opportunity to grow or to, perhaps, prevent a bigger issue from happening, understanding that all difficulties are temporary. Practicing unconditional gratitude will bring more serenity, as we appreciate life, without complaint, when things don't go our way. Be the farmer described in "Acceptance." Choose gratitude, regardless of the circumstances.

Sometimes it's only after a difficult life experience that we can stop denying death and have the realization that we are only passengers on Earth. Life is the most precious gift. Gratitude for what we know or possess is helpful, but these things will eventually be taken from us. What remains is the love we have given. What does life want from us? The answer is simple: It wants us to feel happiness, wholeness, and oneness in the present moment; to use this present opportunity to grow in love and be more aware.

Mother Teresa said, "Be happy in the moment, that's enough. Each moment is all we need, not more." This gratitude for life, breathing and seeing all things as a blessing, is a high spiritual state. We feel truly grateful for every given moment, as an opportunity to love, act with kindness, and be happy. If we see every moment as a gift from life, we will find inner joy.

More positive changes

When we feel more grateful about life experiences, we are more likely to attract positive changes and have a positive perspective. If we focus on the good qualities of our spouse, they will be more loving. If we are grateful for our job, we will be more productive and possibly merit a raise. This is called the grateful circle.

Fewer negative emotions (resentment, frustration, or pride)
Gratitude for what we experience frees us from negative emotions. It reduces the feeling of guilt ("I should be doing something different," or "I should be doing better.").

Gratitude is the antidote for pride. Being prideful is associated with fear of potential loss, anger, and resentment. No one feels comfortable around prideful people, as the circumstances often invite attacks, endless arguments, and humiliation. Pride causes a loss of energy, as we are constantly preoccupied with defending "the truth," according to our relative perception. We defend our lifestyles, jobs, clothes, kids' schools, political views, countries and religious beliefs. It comes as no surprise that when replace this with gratitude, one seeks, instead, to be truthful and to honour our respective differences. With gratitude, we choose to share what we have, rather than being prideful or asking for more.

Studies on Gratitude

Gratitude is associated with many benefits, including better physical, psychological, and social health.
Several studies suggest that gratitude may make people physically healthier, adopt a healthier lifestyle[1-2] and sleep better.[3-5] In general, grateful people are happier and more satisfied with their lives, less materialistic, and less likely to suffer from burnout.[6-11] Grateful people show lower hedonic adaptation—the tendency to return to a relatively stable level of happiness despite major positive or negative events or life changes.[12] Additionally, some studies have found that gratitude practices, like keeping a gratitude journal, or writing a letter of gratitude, can increase people's happiness and overall positive moods.[13-17] People who feel grateful about life experiences, instead of focusing on discontentment, tend to have lower emotional disturbance. Indeed, studies show that gratitude significantly predicts lower levels

of stress and less depression and anxiety symptoms.[18] More studies also suggest that gratitude inspires people to be more prosocial[19] and strengthens relationship.[20]

Ways to Cultivate Gratitude

It may initially feel difficult cultivating gratitude, but this mental state grows stronger with use and practice. Here are some ways to regularly cultivate gratitude:

- Count your blessings. Affirm the goodness in your life and stop discounting the positive.
- Start your day thinking of someone to thank.
- Write a thank-you letter to express appreciation.
- Keep a gratitude journal. Make it a habit to write, or share with a loved one, what you feel grateful for.
- Meditate. You can practice mindfulness meditation, which involves focusing on the present moment, without judgment. Focus on what you're grateful for. (See example of meditation below).
- Pray/Contemplate. Consider practicing prayer or contemplation, recognizing the beauty of life in all forms.
- Don't fall into the trap of thinking "I wish life were different."
- Think of what you already have (80% of the time) instead of what you want (20% of the time).
- Recognize that the source of this goodness is at least partially created outside of yourself.
- Remember that gratitude is not viewing others as worse off than you.

Examples of daily meditation:

Let yourself sit quietly and at ease.

Allow your body, brain, and heart to feel relaxed and unrestricted.

Begin the practice of gratitude, feeling as time passes that you care for your life.

Allow yourself to acknowledge all that has supported you throughout your life.

Now shift your practice to the cultivation of joy. Continue to breathe gently. Bring to mind someone you care about and who is easy to rejoice for. Picture them and feel the natural joy you have for their wellbeing, happiness, and success. With each breath, offer them your grateful, heartfelt wishes:

May you be joyful.

May your happiness increase.

May you not be separated from great happiness.

May your good fortune and the causes for your joy increase.

Practice living in joy until the deliberate effort of repetition drops away, and the intentions of joy blend into the natural joy of your own wise heart.

(Excerpt: *The Wise Heart by Jack Kornfield*)

CHAPTER EIGHT

HOPE

What is Hope?

St. Thomas Aquinas defined it as "a future good, difficult but possible to attain." In psychology, hope also refers to something in the future; it implies the existence of a goal, combined with a plan for reaching that goal. Hope is not merely wishful thinking, but an active process that involves commitment, whereas wishing is passive. Carl Jung wrote, "Faith, hope, love, and insight are the highest achievements of human effort. They are found and given by experience."

While no one is exempt from experiencing challenging life events, hope fosters an orientation to life that allows a grounded and optimistic outlook, even in the most demanding of circumstances. According to Hope Theory, as proposed by Professor Rick Snyder, hope comprises three components:

1. **Goals:** Having goals you feel invested in, such as having a loving family, finding a life partner, or achieving success.

2. **Agency:** Believing you have the ability to achieve your goals and overcome obstacles.

3. **Pathways:** Finding multiple, potential pathways to achieve your goals.

Goals are not contradictory to spiritual growth; the issue is when we become attached to them. Holding goals in your mind is inspirational and helpful, for accomplishment, because what you hold tends to manifest. What you truly need is to let go of the desire and expectation behind any goal. One can hope for something and, at the same time, surrender to life and God, no matter how things turn out. It may be useful to pray for the highest good, in any situation, and trust that everything will work-out for the best in the end. Remember that at the end, no matter how difficult the path may be, what life wants from you is to grow in love and consciousness, even in the midst of chaos. Life wants your happiness, oneness, and wholeness.

It is worth mentioning, that as you grow spiritually, your goals tend to be based on more intuition and feelings, rather than egoistic thinking. The need for money, fame, prestige, power, competitiveness, esteem, and safety diminishes and is replaced by motivations of love, compassion, kindness, cooperation, freedom, creativity, and spiritual awakening. When this happens, our goals are no longer positioned towards selfish desires, but towards the wellbeing of all.

Types of Hope

Words like hope may appear vague in meaning, as there are many ways to think about it. Let's examine some of the most common types of hope we can experience.(1)

Realistic Hope

This is the standard perspective, for an outcome that is reasonable or probable. It allows us to observe and understand a situation, while still maintaining openness, towards the possibility of positive change.

Utopian Hope

Utopian hope is a collectively oriented hope that refers to collaborative action, which can lead to a better future for all. You can consider the permaculture movement an example of utopian hope, where a civilization, built using permaculture design and Earth Care ethics, strives for a better future. As co-founder of the movement, Bill Mollison, said "Sitting at our back doorsteps, all we need to live a good life lies about us. Sun, wind, people, buildings, stones, sea, birds, and plants surround us. Cooperation with all these things brings harmony; opposition to them brings disaster and chaos."

Borrowed Hope

The hope one can borrow from others or community. People who experience more hope can share this positive energy with those who are downcast. Sometimes another person sees cause for hope more easily than you can. If the person is honest and trustworthy, you can borrow their confidence *in* you, as well as their hope *for* you. Support is a critical factor, in the development of any type of hope. While an absence of support can lead to isolation, hopelessness, and lack of motivation, an individual with a solid support network is better able to imagine positive possibilities.

Transcendent (Spiritual) Hope

Transcendent hope refers to general hopefulness, not tied to a specific outcome or goal. This can be expressed as a general attitude of hopefulness, while refusing to imagine or define the future. It can also be interpreted as things working out for the best, however even if they don't, then it's not the end of the world.

It is sometimes during "the dark night of the soul" that transcendent hope can be found. As Sufi mystic, Rumi, said, "Where there is ruin, there is hope for a treasure." We often feel ruined by what is happening in our lives or in the world around us. Ruined by all the things we wished had happened, but never did, or ruined by our thoughts of hopelessness, despair, and depression. Yet, it is during these moments, of great despair, that we can discover this highest hope—that there is something greater within us, that has the power to sustain us, no matter how hard the experience feels.

Inborn Hope

This refers to the "innate hope" within us, the inherent part of being a human being. It is in a child's basic disposition to carry hope, unless adults do something to threaten it, or there is a genetic predisposition to depression and hopelessness.

Unrealistic Hope

Often referred to as false hope, it is based on unrealistic expectations. The principal areas, in which expectations tend to be unrealistic, fall within the speed, amount, ease, and effect of changes, in one's own life. We might have false hope that one person, whether it be a friend or spouse, can meet all of our needs and make us unendingly happy.

Chosen Hope

This can be defined as choosing hope, over negative emotions, in a response to undesirable experiences or the uncertain future. In the context of palliative care, hopeful people, in advanced stages of cancer, set limited goals relating to their quality of life or choose to say goodbye to family members.

Benefits of Hope

Hope is positively related to overall life satisfaction.[(2)] Hopeful people tend to have greater physical and psychological wellbeing, good self-esteem, and enriched interpersonal relationships.[(3)] Individuals with high hope are more likely to view stressful situations as challenging rather than threatening, which is a beneficially protective outlook against stress[(4)] and anxiety.[(5)]

Hope is a motivational factor that helps initiate and sustains action toward long-term goals.[(6)] It motivates individuals to maintain their positive involvement in life regardless of limitations imposed upon them.[(7)] The interesting fact is that when hope results in positive outcomes, an upward spiral is created, in which good results lead to increased hope, and more hope leads to continued success.

EXERCISE:

How would you describe having *hope?*

How does hope benefit your life?

In your opinion, how does a person that has hope, look and sound like?

How have you used hope in your own life?

Do you believe having hope carries risks?

If a picture on your wall made you feel hopeful every morning, what would that picture show?

What small changes could build hope for you?

What Can I Do to Be More Hopeful?

Focus on one or more areas of life.

Work on areas of life that are most meaningful to you. They may involve things like prioritizing healthy living, the pursuit of spirituality, being a better parent/partner, or making contributions to your family and community.

Set Clear and Specific Goals.

After defining an area of significant importance, set noticeably clear and specific goals within that area. A helpful approach would be the use of the SMART acronym: Specific, Measurable, Achievable, Realistic, and Timely.(8) Goals that include these features are more likely to be achieved. For example, if you live far from your family, and family is important to you, consider setting the goal of a one-hour Zoom call each week, with family members.

S – *Specific*: keep your goals specific and narrow your focus, for more effective planning.

M – *Measurable:* identify what evidence will demonstrate progress, then re-evaluate as needed.

A – *Attainable/Achievable*: make sure your goals can be accomplished within a reasonable timeframe.

R – *Realistic/Relevant*: Align your goals with your values and long-term objectives.

T – *Time Bound:* Set a realistically ambitious end-date for task prioritization and motivation.

Set Goals That Relate to Each Other.

Set a series of goals that systematically build on top of each other. If you want your children to have a wisdom-based education that honors not only intellect but also intuitiveness (creativity, imagination, nature, art, and values such as unconditional love), you might involve your children in activities that emphasize intuition. This can be followed-up with the goal of having them share their new skill with the community.

Set Goals Related to Things You Can Control and Accept Things You Can't Control.

The Serenity Prayer is a useful tool. Remember, it's helpful to set realistic goals that are within your control, while also acknowledging how much of the end result is actually within your control.

Be flexible.

Continue to revisit and re-evaluate your goals. Think about what obstacles you are likely to face and continue to generate creative solutions. Stay flexible and change plans when repeated efforts don't work. Ask for help, from those that possess experience and/or wisdom that can benefit you.

Use Your Desired Outcome as a Source of Motivation

Regularly visualize or think about your desired future achievement. If you want to start a regular meditation routine, envision how much better you will feel while meditating. Avoid wishful thinking. Instead, take action to accomplish this goal.

EXERCISE:

> Worksheet – according to the book entitled, *Hope Rising: How the Science of Hope Can Change Your Life*:[13]
>
> *(Describe a goal with as much detail as possible.)*

How much desire do you have to meet your goal?

Discuss your reasons for wanting to achieve this goal. List what is motivating you.

Describe how you will feel if your goal is achieved.

List the pathways (actions/strategies) you can use to achieve your goal.

Describe potential barriers for each pathway listed.

Choose the best path and explain how you will overcome these barriers.

What are two or three things that must be accomplished before attaining your goal?

Identify people and/or resources you can rely on, for support in pursuit of your goal.

Describe what motivates/inspires you (e.g., music, a movie, a person, etc.).

Hope and Religions

In major world religions, people often refer to "transcendent hope." It exists without connection to external circumstances and this type of hope gives people the power to continue moving forward, even when they stumble. It also provides the motivation, to never give up, regardless of the situation.

Consider a few inspiring quotes, regarding hope:

> *Do not lose heart nor fall into despair! You shall triumph if you are believers.*
> (Quran 3:139)
>
> *After a difficulty, Allah will soon grant relief.* (Quran 65:7)
>
> *And we know that all things work together for the good of those that love God, to those who are called according to His purpose.* (Romans 8:28)
>
> *The power of God is with you at all times; through the activities of mind, senses, breathing, and emotions and is constantly doing all the work using you as a mere instrument.* (The Bhagavad Gita)
>
> *Every experience, no matter how bad it seems, holds within it a blessing of some kind. The goal is to find it.* (Buddha)

The ultimate hope and faith in major religions is to reach the kingdom of God/Heaven" or Enlightenment through spirituality. The source of this hope is connected to a Living Presence within. It is the spring at the bottom of the well of our being through which hope, love, and joy are continually renewed. The good news shared by Jesus is that "the kingdom of God is within you." One is called upon to awaken to this truth, to go beyond the ego and find the ultimate reality, here and now, present within. The hope and faith within lets us know there is something greater than death and suffering. When Jesus stopped at the well to ask the Samaritan woman for a drink of water, he spoke of this hope. "Everyone who drinks this water will be thirsty again, but whoever drinks the water I will give him will never thirst. Indeed, the water I give him will become in him a spring of water welling up to eternal life" (John 4:13-14).

Muslim Sufi, Rumi, stated: "The river that flows in you also flows in me," meaning that in the depth of our being we all have access to the same source of love, joy, and hope.

Suicide and Hopelessness

Suicide is an act of despair, most commonly caused by the loss of hope and faith. If we lose all hope for the future, we may mistakenly think suicide is a solution. We may experience tunnel vision when, in the middle of a crisis, we believe suicide is the only way out. It is important to understand that suicide is rarely caused by a single factor, and there are numerous means of prevention.

Risk factors of suicide.[9-10]

Hopelessness

History of previous suicide attempts – attempted suicide is more frequent for women, and men are more likely, than women, to succeed.

Psychiatric disorders – major depression, post-traumatic stress disorder, or bipolar disorder. Ninety percent of patients who attempt suicide have a psychiatric disorder.

Substance abuse

Marital status – suicide occurs more often among people who are not married than those who are married.

Socially isolated

Sexual minority – lesbian, gay, bisexual, or transgender individuals, with an unsupportive family or in a hostile environment.

Medical illnesses – suicide risk increases with chronic disease, chronic pain, or terminal illness.

Childhood adversity – the risk of suicide attempts is two to four times greater in adults who suffered childhood abuse or other adverse childhood experiences (e.g, physical neglect).

Family history and genetics – the risk of suicide increases in patients with a family history of suicide, mental disorders, or substance abuse.

Firearms – access to firearms in your home.

Media reporting – studies have shown that suicide rates can increase up to 13% after a celebrities' suicide.

Antidepressants – Antidepressants carry the warning that they are associated with an increased risk of suicidality, in adults ages 18 to 24, during initial treatment (generally, the first one to two months).

Stressful life event – the loss of a loved one, a breakup, or financial or legal problems.

Suicide warning signs[11]

Talking about suicide – "I wish I were dead" or "I wish I hadn't been born."

Giving away belongings or getting affairs in order, with no other logical explanation for doing so.

Saying goodbye to people as if they won't see them again.

Buying a gun or stockpiling pills.

Withdrawing from social contacts.

Being preoccupied with death, dying, or violence.

Doing risky or self-destructive things, such as using drugs or driving recklessly.

Worsening of psychiatric problems or addiction.

Prevention[12]

Get the treatment you need – All illnesses are physical, mental, social, and spiritual in origin, and the most successful way to recover is by simultaneously addressing all of these areas.

Establish your support network – Friends and family, places of worship, support groups, or other community resources.

Don't cope with suicidal thoughts or behavior on your own.

Take medications as directed – Do *not* abruptly stop taking a prescribed antidepressant or any other medication.

Learn about your condition – With depression, for instance, read about its symptoms, causes, and treatments.

Pay attention to warning signs – Work with your doctor or therapist, to learn what triggers your suicidal feelings.

Have a plan of action to follow if/when suicidal thoughts return – Clearly state your suicidal intention, with your therapist.

Get rid of any potential means with which to kill yourself – Firearms, knives, or dangerous medications.

Seek help from a support group – Several organizations are available to help you cope with suicidal thoughts and to help you recognize that there are many options, other than suicide.

ASIST – Applied Suicide Intervention Skills Training (ASIST) is a two-day interactive workshop in suicide first-aid.

EXERCISE:

What would you say to a suicidal friend?

COMMENTS

Knowing the seven principles is like knowing the truth about happiness. It is the key which can free you from many limitations, boundaries, and conflicts…No matter where you are in life, you will find something meaningful and of great value by practicing these principles. I have seen profound transformations when my patients, colleagues, and I began applying these principles in our daily lives. They are simple yet powerful. Devote yourself to them and transform yourself and your relationships with loved ones and everyone around you.

Mehwish Hanif, MD, CCFP
Family Physician
Clinical Lecturer | Department of Family Medicine, University of Calgary
Cofounder of the Soul Program

***

In my clinical practice, I have often highlighted Non-Attachment ("be OK with or without"), and Acceptance ("God, grant me the serenity to accept the things I cannot change, courage to change the things I can, and wisdom to know the difference") for my mental-health patients. In retrospect, I believe it's because these two principles resonated with me personally and comforted me greatly in challenging times.

Experiencing the COVID-19 pandemic, we confirmed, or, for the first time, realized the fragility of our society and our definition of normalcy. We encountered many instances of powerlessness as we foraged the unknown territory of overwhelming instability (including ever-changing policy, by-laws, further social isolation, and even loss of our loved ones). In navigating these uncertain times, we experienced degrees of frustration, devastation, and hopelessness. In such times, I felt that the seven principles, especially the two mentioned above, were solid foundations that gave me the energy to carry on with hope.

Dr. TaeEun Ahn, MSc, MD, CCFP
Family Physician
Clinical Lecturer | Department of Family Medicine, University of Calgary
Cofounder of the Soul Program

***

Dr. Nader Attalla's seven principles utilizes a multi-faith approach to universalize core elements of the human experience. Each principle carefully links to the next to create a roadmap for self-discovery, with the ultimate goal of living as one's authentic self. By following the principles, one can attain peace and harmony within oneself and with those around them.

Dr. Magdalene Leung, MSc, MD, CCFP
Family Physician
Cofounder of the Soul Program

***

I have witnessed, first hand, how the principles, taught by Dr. Attalla, have changed patient's and professionals mindsets and lives. All seven principles are significant and serve us and others well, when used appropriately and applied often. Each one compliments and works harmoniously with the others, to provide balance, purpose and peace in our lives. They are uncomplicated reminders of how to find value in ourselves and nature and leave others better than how we found them. The ones most impactful to me are Non-Attachment, Acceptance, and Powerlessness. I love the idea that *we will be ok, with or without*, in all situations, despite what or who we have or don't have. This idea that our happiness is not dependant on "things," but how we choose to embrace life…The principle of Acceptance is also beautiful, in the sense that we believe others, despite their behaviour, are trying their best, with the tools they have and experiences they've had. This thinking removes blame and frees us to assume the best of people. Powerlessness is important because, regardless of your perspective on religion or spirituality, you can surrender your burdens to something bigger than yourself, which is humbling and freeing.

Brooklyn Harrington, RSW
Group Co-Facilitator
Cofounder of the Soul Program

***

It is an honour to contribute to the realization of this book with the information gathered from Dr. Attalla's seminars about the seven principles. The book offers practical intervention that will serve patients as well as clinicians in integrating spirituality and mental health. It is a great reminder of how to undo our wounded egos and inspire the integration of our highest virtues, such as Unconditional Love, Acceptance, Non-Judgment, Gratitude, Powerlessness, Hope, and Faith. In practicing these spiritual principles, I was personally able to give meaning to my own difficulties…My suffering was an occasion for deep transformation, a movement toward wholeness and inner peace. And in true humility, this is a lifetime path. As a new mother blessed with a child after many years of infertility struggles, these spiritual principles will serve me for the rest of my life. Nobody is exempt from suffering, but we can all make it an occasion to grow. Rather than simply be given a prescription and diagnosis, we need tools to balance our bio-psycho-social and spiritual health. The goal of the therapist is to offer the best conditions so that our true nature can operate. Dr. Nader Attalla is a true doctor of the soul…I am grateful for this book, which gives practical tools to guide us back to wholeness, and for his devotion to the wellbeing of all.

Mélissa Vallières, RN

***

The Seven Principles, in which Dr. Attalla bases his methods of healing and self-awareness, have a place in every being's life. No matter age, gender, religious belief, or background, each principle will resonate... and improve one's quality of life greatly when practiced. One may find gratitude will flow naturally as a by-product of practicing the other six... Unconditional Love and Non-Judgement enables one to let go of a need to control others and see that all of us harbour good and not-so-good qualities. They enable us to be OK and press forward despite the hurt or disappointment...as a result of another's actions. We also can have boundaries whilst loving unconditionally!
The ever-pressing journey to continuously surrender to life's hurdles and triumphs is supported through Non-Attachment and Acceptance. Personally, these two principles (...also supported by the legendary Dr. David Hawkins) may be the toughest I will work on throughout my life, but if I/we do not, there is more likelihood of becoming psychologically stuck in the inevitabilities of life.
I hope everyone that comes across a copy of this book takes the time to read and reflect, as it will create a personal paradigm shift for the better.

Catrina

***

When I am lacking in the principle of Non-Attachment, whether I'm attached to a person, an ideal of that person, an expectation, a hope for something I have no control over, or a wish that things could be different...the attachment alone creates almost debilitating anxiety. Anxiety that makes it difficult to concentrate on anything...let alone live a productive life. When I can move myself to a place of non-attachment and accept that things are what they are, and the future will be what it is meant to be, I find peace and the ability to live my life more freely.

Sonja

***

How the seven principles helped me in my personal life and contributed to the journey towards recovery:

1. Non-attachment: My career as a bookkeeper defined me for decades. Upon retirement, there was a void in my sense of self. Over the last eleven years, I have learned that there was much more that described me as an individual...

2. Acceptance: I had more difficulty learning to accept people than situations or events. I thought that either people should change, or I could change them. Neither is possible; accepting people the way they are (good and bad) is the only way I can effectively get along with them.

3. Non-judgement: The best tool I have to help not judge those around me is to put myself in their shoes. Just because my addiction has not left me homeless does not give me the right to look down on those who are. Everybody has a story, and I know the names of some of the people who collect bottles in my alley. Acknowledging them with a smile is good for both of us.

4. Gratitude: One of the things I am most grateful for is our robust health-care system. Other than a few glitches along the way, it has saved me from dying from HIV and enabled my partner to have brain surgery. I do put in much effort to navigate and access the system.

5. Hope: The light at the end of the tunnel is my mantra for recovery. Though I can barely stay sober for three weeks, the skills I am learning from therapy and pharmaceutical help give me hope. Without them, I would surely die of alcoholism.

6. Unconditional Love: I receive unconditional love from my two dogs and give it in return. This model is so simple that it is easy to extrapolate to my partner and eventually to all those around me. Deistically, I am focusing on my partner and family first, then my friends and acquaintances.

7. Powerlessness: The concept of powerlessness has two dimensions for me. First is that over alcohol, as stated in Step One of Alcoholics

Anonymous. It is the unmanageability of my life that I have trouble defining. The second is my powerlessness over people, places, and things. Once I realised that I have little or no influence over most of everything that goes on in the world, the path to surrender became much more visible and uncluttered.

Gordon

***

I have been a patient of Dr. Attalla for three years. I first sought treatment due to my battle with anxiety which, at times, was debilitating. Working with Dr. Attalla and learning the seven spiritual principles as part of my therapy has given me the tools to help experience a more deeply gratifying life.

One of the greatest challenges at the beginning…was being too tied to the outcome of situations. As I learned about Non-Attachment and applied it to my life, I felt myself becoming OK to be with or without. My periods of anxiety started to decrease, and the acceptance of my powerlessness began to grow.

I am incredibly grateful to Dr. Attalla for his loving guidance, support, and encouragement. As I learn to adopt and apply each of these seven principles, I am drawn closer to my higher power and filled with the unconditional love that is needed to live life to the full.

Terry

***

REFERENCES

Chapter One

1. H.G. Koenig, D.E. King, and V.B. Carson, *Handbook of Religion and Health*, Oxford University Press, New York, NY, USA, 2nd edition, 2012.

2. Exercise for Mental Health: 8 Keys to Get and Stay Moving. National Alliance on Mental Illness. https://www.nami.org/Blogs/NAMI-Blog/May-2016/Exercise-for-Mental-Health-8-Keys-to-Get-and-Stay. Accessed Sept. 7, 2017.

3. Zschucke E, et al,. Exercise and Physical Activity in Mental Disorders: Clinical and Experimental Evidence. *Journal of Preventive Medicine and Public Health*. 2013;46:512.

4. Anderson E, et al., Effects of Exercise and Physical Activity on Anxiety. Frontiers in Psychiatry. 2013;4:1.

5. Sleep Hygiene Tips. Centers for Disease Control and Prevention. https://www.cdc.gov/sleep/about_sleep/sleep_hygiene.html. Accessed April 7, 2017.

6. Jagannath, A., Taylor, L., Wakaf, Z., Vasudevan, S.R., & Foster, R.G. (2017). The Genetics of Circadian Rhythms, Sleep and Health. *Human Molecular Genetics,* 26(R2), R128–R138. https://doi.org/10.1093/hmg/ddx240

7. Academy of Nutrition and Dietetics: Inflammation and Diet.

8. H.G. Koenig, Religion, Spirituality, and Health: The Research and Clinical Implications, International Scholarly Research Notices, ISRN Psychiatry, 2012.

9. L. Tepper, S.A. Rogers, E.M. Coleman, and H.N. Malony, The Prevalence of Religious Coping Among Persons with

Persistent Mental Illness, *Psychiatric Services*, vol. 52, no. 5, pp. 660–665, 2001.

10. Krause N., Religious Meaning and Subjective Well-Being in Late Life. *Journals of Gerontology Series B, Volume 58, Issue 3, May* 2003;58(3):S160–S170. [PubMed] [Google Scholar]

11. Murphy, P.E., Ciarrocchi, J.W., Piedmont R.L., Cheston S., Peyrot M., Fitchett G., The Relation of Religious Belief and Practices, Depression, and Hopelessness in Persons with Clinical Depression. *Journal of Consulting and Clinical Psychology.* 2000;68(6):1102–1106. [PubMed] [Google Scholar]

12. . N. Le, W. Tov, and J. Taylor, Religiousness and Depressive Symptoms in Five Ethnic Adolescent Groups, *International Journal for the Psychology of Religion*, vol. 17, no. 3, pp. 209–232, 2007. View at: Google Scholar

13. Skrabski, A., Kopp, M., Rózsa, S., Réthelyi, J., Rahe, R.H., Life Meaning: An Important Correlate of Health in the Hungarian Population. *International Journal of Behavioral Medicine.* 2005;12(2):78–85. [PubMed] [Google Scholar]

14. Krause N., God-Mediated Control and Change in Self-Rated Health. *International Journal for the Psychology of Religion.* 2010;20(4):267–287. [PMC free article] [PubMed] [Google Scholar]

15. Saroglou, V., Pichon, I., Trompette, L., Verschueren, M., Dernelle, R., Prosocial Behavior and Religion: New Evidence Based on Projective Measures and Peer Ratings. *Journal for the Scientific Study of Religion.* 2005;44(3):323–348. [Google Scholar]

16. N. Krause and C.G. Ellison, Forgiveness by God, Forgiveness of Others, and Psychological Well-Being in Late Life, *Journal for the Scientific Study of Religion*, vol. 42, no. 1, pp. 77–93, 2003. View at: Publisher Site | Google Scholar

17. Toussaint, L.L., Marschall, J.C., Williams, D.R., Prospective Associations Between Religiousness/Spirituality and Depression and Mediating Effects of Forgiveness in a Nationally Representative Sample of United States Adults. *Depression Research and Treatment.* 2012;2012:10 pages.267820 [PMC free article] [PubMed] [Google Scholar]

18. Krause, N., Religious Involvement, Gratitude, and Change in Depressive Symptoms Over Time. *International Journal for the Psychology of Religion.* 2009;19(3):155–172. [PMC free article] [PubMed] [Google Scholar]

19. Steffen, P.R., Masters, K.S. Does Compassion Mediate the Intrinsic Religion-Health Relationship? *Annals of Behavioral Medicine.* 2005;30(3):217–224. [PubMed] [Google Scholar]

20. L. Miller, R. Bansai, P. Wickramaratne, X. Hao, C.E. Tenke, and M.M. Weissman, Neuroanatomical Correlates of Religiosity and Spirituality: A Study in Adults at High and Low Familial Risk for Depression (forthcoming), 2014. View at: Google Scholar

21. S. Kasen, P., Wickramaratne, and M.J. Gameroff, Religiosity and Resilience in Persons at High Risk for Major Depression, *Psychological Medicine*, vol. 42, no. 3, pp. 509–519, 2012. View at: Google Scholar

22. T. Rasic, S.L., Belik, B., Elias, L.Y., Katz, M., Enns, and Sareen, J., Spirituality, Religion and Suicidal Behavior in a Nationally Representative Sample, *Journal of Affective Disorders*, vol. 114, no. 1-3, pp. 32–40, 2009. View at: [PubMed] [Ref list]

23. B. Wachholtz and K.I. Pargament, Migraines and Meditation: Does Spirituality Matter? *Journal of Behavioral Medicine*, vol. 31, no. 4, pp. 351–366, 2008. View at: Publisher Site | Google Scholar

24. E. Foley, A. Baillie, M. Huxter, M. Price, and E. Sinclair,

Mindfulness-Based Cognitive Therapy for Individuals Whose Lives Have Been Affected by Cancer: A Randomized Controlled Trial, *Journal of Consulting and Clinical Psychology*, vol. 78, no. 1, pp. 72–79, 2010. View at: Publisher Site | Google Scholar
M. D. Regnerus and G. H. Elder, Religion and Vulnerability Among Low-Risk Adolescents, *Social Science Research*, vol. 32, no. 4, pp. 633–658, 2003. View at: Publisher Site | Google Scholar

25. M.E. Pagano, S.E. Zemore, C.C. Onder, and R.L. Stout, Predictors of Initial AA-Related Helping: Findings from Project MATCH, *Journal of Studies on Alcohol and Drugs*, vol. 70, no. 1, pp. 117–125, 2009. [PubMed] [Ref list]

26. T.A. Wills, A.M. Yaeger, and J.M. Sandy, Buffering Effect of Religiosity for Adolescent Substance Use, *Psychology of Addictive Behaviors*, vol. 17, no. 1, pp. 24–31, 2003. View at: Publisher Site | Google Scholar

27. W.J. Strawbridge, S.J. Shema, R.D. Cohen, and G.A. Kaplan, Religious Attendance Increases Survival by Improving and Maintaining Good Health Behaviors, Mental Health, and Social Relationships, *Annals of Behavioral Medicine*, vol. 23, no. 1, pp. 68–74, 2001. View at: Google Scholar

28. N. Krause and E. Bastida, Core Religious Beliefs and Providing Support to Others in Late Life, *Mental Health, Religion and Culture*, vol. 12, no. 1, pp. 75–96, 2009. View at: Publisher Site | Google Scholar

29. H.G. Koenig, *Religion and Mental Health Research and Application*, Academic Press, USA, 2018.

Chapter Two

1. Sahdra B., Shaver P., Brown K. (2010). A Scale to Measure Nonattachment: a Buddhist Complement to Western Research

on Attachment Adaptive Functioning. J. Pers. Assess. 92, 116–127. 10.1080/00223890903425960

2. Whitehead R., Bates G., Elphinstone B., Yang Y., Murray G. (2018). Nonattachment Mediates the Relationship of Mindfulness to Psychological and Subjective Well-Being, Depression, Anxiety and Stress. *J. Happiness Stud.* 10.1007/s10902-018-0041-9 [CrossRef] [Google Scholar]

3. Sahdra, B.K., Ciarrochi, J., Parker, P.D., Marshall, S., and Heaven, P. (2015). Empathy and Nonattachment Independently Predict Peer Nominations of Prosocial Behavior of Adolescents. *Frontiers in Psychology, 6,* 263–292. http://dx.doi.org/10.3389/fpsyg.2015.00263

4. Bradshaw, Matt, Ellison, Christopher G., and Marcum, Jack P. (2010). Attachment to God, Images of God, and Psychological Distress in a Nationwide Sample of Presbyterians. *International Journal for the Psychology of Religion* 20:130–47.

5. Ellison C.G., Bradshaw, M, Flannelly K.J., Galek, K.C. Prayer, Attachment to God, and Symptoms of Anxiety-Related Disorders Among U.S. Adults. *Sociology of Religion* 2014; 75:208–233.

6. Worthington, E.L., Jr., Hook, J.N, Utsey, S.O, Williams, J.K., Neil, R.L. Decisional and Emotional Forgiveness. Paper presented at the International Positive Psychology Summit; Washington, DC 2007.

7. Toussaint, L.L., Shields, G.S., Slavich, G.M. Forgiveness, Stress, and Health: A 5-Week Dynamic Parallel Process Study. *Ann Behav Med.* 2016;50(5):727–735

8. Thompson, L.Y., Snyder, C., Hoffman, L., et al. Dispositional Forgiveness of Self, Others, and Situations. *J Pers.* 2005;73(2):313–360.

9. Lawler, K.A., Younger, J.W., Piferi, R.L., Jobe, R.L., Edmondson, K.A., Jones, W.H. The Unique Effects of Forgiveness on Health: An Exploration of Pathways. *J Behav Med.* 2005;28(2):157–167.

10. Lin, W.F., Mack, D., Enright, R.D., Krahn, D., Baskin, T.W. Effects of Forgiveness Therapy on Anger, Mood, and Vulnerability to Substance Use Among Inpatient Substance-Dependent Clients. *J Consult Clin Psychol.* 2004;72(6):1114–1121.

11. Akhtar, S., Barlow, J. Forgiveness Therapy for the Promotion of Mental Well-Being: A Systematic Review and Meta-Analysis. *Trauma Violence Abus.* 2018;19(1):107–122.

12. Reed, G.L., Enright, R.D. The Effects of Forgiveness Therapy on Depression, Anxiety, and Posttraumatic Stress for Women After Spousal Emotional Abuse. *Journal of Consulting and Clinical Psychology*. (2006). 74(5):920–929

Chapter Three

1. Hayes, S.C., Luoma, J.B., Bond, F.W., Masuda, A., and Lillis, J. (2006). Acceptance and Commitment Therapy: Model, Processes and Outcomes. *Behav. Res. Ther.* 44, 1–25. doi: 10.1016/j.brat.2005.06.006

2. Twohig, M.P., and Levin, M.E. (2017). Acceptance and Commitment Therapy as a Treatment for Anxiety and Depression: A Review. *Psychiatric Clin.* 40, 751–770. doi: 10.1016/j.psc.2017.08.009

3. Feliu-Soler, A., Montesinos, F., Gutiérrez-Martínez, O., Scott, W., McCracken, L.M., and Luciano, J.V. (2018). Current Status of Acceptance and Commitment Therapy for Chronic Pain: A Narrative Review. *J. Pain Res.* 11:2145. doi: 10.2147/JPR.S144631

4. Veehof, M.M., Oskam, M.-J., Schreurs, K. M.G., and Bohlemeijer, E.T. (2011). Acceptance-Based Interventions for Treatment of Chronic Pain: A Systematic Review and Meta-Analysis. *Pain* 152, 533–542. Doi: 10.1016/j.pain.2010.11.002

5. Cramer, H., Lauche, R., Haller, H., Langhorst, J., and Dobos, G. (2016). Mindfulness-and Acceptance-Based Interventions for Psychosis: A Systematic Review and Meta-Analysis. *Glob. Adv. Health Med.* 5, 30–43. doi: 10.7453/gahmj.2015.083

6. Jansen, J.E., Gleeson, J., Bendall, S., Rice, S., and Alvarez-Jimenez, M. (2019). Acceptance-and Mindfulness-Based Interventions for Persons with Psychosis: A Systematic Review and Meta-Analysis. *Schizophr. Res.* S0920-9964(19)30522-5. doi: 10.1016/j.schres.2019.11.016

7. Prefit, A.B., Cândea, D.M., and Szentagotai-Tătar, A. (2019). Emotion Regulation Across Eating Pathology: A Meta-Analysis. *Appetite* 143:104438. doi: 10.1016/j.appet.2019.104438

8. Lew-Starowicz, M., Lewczuk, K., Nowakowska, I., Kraus, S., and Gola, M. (2019). Compulsive Sexual Behavior and Dysregulation of Emotion. *Sex. Med. Rev.* S2050-0521(19)30103-9. doi: 10.1016/j.sxmr.2019.10.003

9. Bowen, S., Chawla, N., and Marlatt, G.A. (2011). *Mindfulness-Based Relapse Prevention for Addictive Behaviors: A Clinician's Guide*. New York, NY: Guilford Press.

10. Tighe, J., Nicholas, J., Shand, F., and Christensen, H. (2018). Efficacy of Acceptance and Commitment Therapy in Reducing Suicidal Ideation and Deliberate Self-Harm: Systematic Review. *JMIR Mental Health* 5:e10732. doi: 10.2196/10732

11. Aldao, A., Nolen-Hoeksema, S., and Schweizer, S. (2010). Emotion-Regulation Strategies across Psychopathology: A Meta-Analytic Review. *Clin. Psychol. Rev.* 30, 217–237. doi: 10.1016/j.cpr.2009.11.004

Chapter Four

1. Leloup, J.Y. Encounter in the Desert, *In:* Albin Michel (ed.), *Judas and Jesus*. Inner Traditions International, 2007, pp. 134-135.

2. Keng, S.L., Smoski, M.J., and Robins, C.J. Effects of Mindfulness on Psychological Health: A Review of Empirical Studies. *Clinical Psychol Review*, 2011, 31(6): 1041–1056. doi:10.1016/j.cpr.2011.04.006.

3. Brown K.W., Ryan R.M. The Benefits of Being Present: Mindfulness and Its Role in Psychological Well-Being. *Journal of Personality and Social Psychology.* 2003, 84:822–848.

4. Cash, M., Whittingham K. What Facets of Mindfulness Contribute to Psychological Well-Being and Depressive, Anxious, and Stress-Related Symptomatology? *Mindfulness.* 2010, 1:177–182.

5. Dekeyser, M., Raes, F., Leijssen, M., Leysen, S., Dewulf, D. Mindfulness Skills and Interpersonal Behaviour. *Personality and Individual Differences.* 2008; 44:1235–1245.

6. Hofmann, S.G., Sawyer, A.T., Witt, A.A., Oh, D. The Effect of Mindfulness-Based Therapy on Anxiety and Depression: A Meta-Analytic Review. *J Consult Clin Psychol. 2010 Apr; 78(2):169-83.*

Chapter Five

1. Hofmann, S.G., Grossman, P., & Hinton, D.E. (2011). Loving-Kindness and Compassion Meditation: Potential for Psychological Interventions. *Clinical Psychology Review*, 31, 1126–1132.

2. Beauregard, M., Courtemanche J., Paquette, V., Landry St-Pierre, E. The Neural Basis of Unconditional Love. *Psychiatry Research: Neuroimaging*, 2009, 93–98.

3. Bartels, A., Zeki, S. The Neural Correlates of Maternal and Romantic Love. *Neuroimage* 21, 2004, 1155–1166.

4. Esch, T., Stefano, G.B. The Neurobiological Link Between Compassion and Love. *Neuroscience Research Institute,* 2011, doi: 10.12659/MSM.881441

Chapter Six

1. *Twelve Steps and Twelve Traditions* (1996). New York: Alcoholics Anonymous World Services.

2. *Anonymous (2001). Alcoholics Anonymous: The Story of How Many Thousands of Men and Women Have Recovered from Alcoholism, 4th ed.* A.A. World Services. OCLC 49743393.

3. Bradshaw, M., Ellison, C.G, Flannelly, K.J. Prayer, God Imagery, and Symptoms of Psychopathology. *Journal for the Scientific Study of Religion.* 2008; 47:644-659.

4. Koenig, H.G. *You are my beloved. Really?* Amazon: CreateSpace Publishing Platform, 2016.

5. Exline J.J., Pargament K.I., Grubbs J.B., Yali, A.M. The Religious and Spiritual Struggles Scale: Development and Initial Validation. *Psychology of Religion and Spirituality.* 2014;6(3):208-222

6. Gerber, M.M., Boals, A., Schuettler, D. The Unique Contributions of Positive and Negative Religious Coping to Posttraumatic Growth and PTSD. *Psychology of Religion and*

Spirituality. 2011;3(4):298-307.

7. Silton, N.R., Flannelly, K.J., Galek, K., Ellison, C.G. Beliefs About God and Mental Health Among American Adults. *Journal of Religion and Health*. 2014;53(5):1285-1296.

8. Bradshaw, M., Ellison, C.G., Marcum J.P. Attachment to God, Images of God, and Psychological Distress in a Nationwide Sample of Presbyterians. *International Journal for Psychology of Religion*. 2010;20(2):130-147.

9. Kelly, J.F., Humphreys, K., Ferri, M. Alcoholics Anonymous and Other 12-Step Programs for Alcohol Use Disorder. *Cochrane Database of Systematic Reviews* 2020, Issue 3. Art. No.: CD012880. DOI: 10.1002/14651858.CD012880.pub2.

Chapter Seven

1. Krause, N., and Hayward, R.D. (2014). Hostility, Religious Involvement, Gratitude, and Self-Rated Health in Late Life. Research on Aging, 36(6), 731–752. https://doi. Org/10.1177/0164027513519113

2. Hill, P.L., Allemand, M., and Roberts, B.W. (2013). Examining the pathways between gratitude and self-rated physical health across adulthood. *Personality and Individual Differences*, 54(1), 92–96. https://doi.org/10.1016/j. paid.2012.08.011

3. Mills, P.J., Redwine, L.S., Wilson, K., Pung, M.A., Chinh, K., Greenberg, B.H., . . ., Chopra, D. (2015). The Role of Gratitude in Spiritual Well-being in Asymptomatic Heart Failure Patients. *Spirituality in Clinical Practice*, 2(1), 5–17. https://doi.org/10.1037/scp0000050

4. Ng, M.Y., and Wong, W.-S. (2013). The differential effects of gratitude and sleep on psychological distress in patients with chronic pain. *Journal of Health Psychology*, 18(2), 263–271.

http://dx.doi.org/10.1177/1359105312439733

5. Wood, A.M., Joseph, S., Lloyd, J., and Atkins, S. (2009). Gratitude influences sleep through the mechanism of pre-sleep cognitions. *Journal of Psychosomatic Research*, 66(1), 43–48. https://doi.org/10.1016/j.jpsychores.2008.09.002

6. McCullough, M.E., Emmons, R.A., and Tsang, J.A. (2002). The Grateful Disposition: A Conceptual and Empirical Topography. *Journal of Personality and Social Psychology*, 82(1), 112–127. https://doi.org/10.1037//0022-3514.82.1.112

7. Morgan, B., Gulliford, L., and Kristjánsson, K. (2017). A New Approach to Measuring Moral Virtues: The Multi-Component Gratitude Measure. *Personality and Individual Differences*, 107, 179–189. https://doi.org/10.1016/j.paid.2016.11.044

8. Lambert, N.M., Fincham, F.D., Stillman, T.F., and Dean, L.R. (2009). More Gratitude, Less Materialism: The Mediating Role of Life Satisfaction. *The Journal of Positive Psychology*, 4(1), 32–42. https://doi.org/10.1080/17439760802216311

9. Chan, D.W. (2011). Burnout and Life Satisfaction: Does Gratitude Intervention Make a Difference Among Chinese School Teachers in Hong Kong? *Educational Psychology*, 31(7), 809–823. https://doi.org/10.1080/01443410.2011.608525

10. Lanham, Michelle, E., Rye, Mark, S., Rimsky, Liza, S., and Weill, S. R. (2012). How Gratitude Relates to Burnout and Job Satisfaction in Mental Health Professionals. *Journal of Mental Health Counseling*, 34(4), 341–354. https://doi.org/10.17744/mehc.34.4.w35q80w11kgpqn26

11. Lyubomirsky, S., Sheldon, K.M., and Schkade, D. (2005). Pursuing Happiness: The Architecture of Sustainable Change. *Review of General Psychology*, 9(2), 111–131. https://doi.org/10.1037/1089-2680.9.2.111

12. Emmons, R.A., and McCullough, M. E. (2003). Counting Blessings versus Burdens: An Experimental Investigation of Gratitude and Subjective Well-Being in Daily Life. *Journal of Personality and Social Psychology, 84*(2), 377–389. https://doi.org/10.1037/0022-3514.84.2.377

13. Seligman, M.E.P., Steen, T.A., Park, N., and Peterson, C. (2005). Positive Psychology Progress: Empirical Validation of Interventions. *American Psychologist*, 60(5), 410–421. https://doi.org/10.1037/0003-066X.60.5.410

14. Jackowska, M., Brown, J., Ronaldson, A., and Steptoe, A. (2016). The Impact of a Brief Gratitude Intervention on Subjective Well-Being, Biology and Sleep. *Journal of Health Psychology*, 21(10), 2207–17. https://doi.org/10.1177/1359105315572455

15. Toepfer, S.M., Cichy, K., and Peters, P. (2012). Letters of Gratitude: Further Evidence for Author Benefits. *Journal of Happiness Studies*, 13(1), 187–201. https://doi.org/10.1007/s10902-011-9257-7

16. Wood, A.M., Maltby, J., Gillett, R., Linley, P.A., and Joseph, S. (2008). The Role of Gratitude in the Development of Social Support, Stress, and Depression: Two Longitudinal Studies. *Journal of Research in Personality*, 42(4), 854–871. https://doi. org/10.1016/j.jrp.2007.11.003

17. McCullough, M. E., Emmons, R. A., & Tsang, J.-A. (2002). The grateful disposition: A conceptual and empirical topography. Journal of Personality and Social Psychology, 82(1), 112–127. https://doi.org/10.1037//0022-3514.82.1.112

18. Bartlett, M. Y., Condon, P., Cruz, J., Baumann, J., & Desteno, D. (2012). Gratitude: Prompting behaviours that build relationships. Cognition & Emotion, 26(1), 2–13. https://doi.org/10.1080/02699931.2011.561297

Chapter Eight

1. Eaves, E.R., Nichter, M., and Ritenbaugh, C. (2016). Ways of Hoping: Navigating the Paradox of Hope and Despair in Chronic Pain. *Culture, Medicine and Psychiatry,* 40(1), 35–58. doi:10.1007/s11013-015-9465-4

2. Roesch, S.C., and Vaughn, A.A. (2006). Evidence for the factorial validity of the dispositional hope scale: Cross-ethnic and cross-gender measurement equivalence. *European Journal of Psychological Assessment,* 22, 78-84.

3. Rand, K.L., and Cheavens, J.S. (2012). Hope Theory. In S.J. Lopez & C.R. Snyder (Eds.), *The Oxford Handbook of Positive Psychology*. London: OUP.

4. Lazarus, R.S. and Launier, R. (1978). Stress-Related Transactions between Person and Environment. In L.A. Pervin and M. Lewis (Eds.), *Perspectives in Interactional Psychology*. New York: Plenum Press.

5. Michael, S.T. (2000). Hope Conquers Fear. In C. Richard Snyder (Ed.), *Handbook of Hope: Theory, Measures, and Applications.* London: Academic Press.

6. Conti, R. (2000). College Goals: Do Self-Determined and Carefully Considered Goals Predict Intrinsic Motivation, Academic Performance, and Adjustment During the First Semester? *Social Psychology of Education, 4, 189–211.*

7. Rideout, E. and Montemuro, M. (1986). Hope, Morale and Adaptation. *Journal of Advanced Nursing,* Vol. 11. doi.org/10.1111/j.1365-2648.1986.tb01270.x

8. Doran, G.T. (1981). "There's a S.M.A.R.T. way to write management's goals and objectives". *Management Review*. 70 (11): 35–36.

Schreiber J, et al. Suicidal ideation and behavior in adults. https://www.uptodate.com/contents/search. Accessed 2021.
Kennebeck S, et al. Suicidal ideation and behavior in children and adolescents: Evaluation and management. https://www.uptodate.com/contents/search. Accessed Jan 1, 2021.
Risk factors and warning signs. American Foundation for Suicide Prevention. https://afsp.org/about-suicide/risk-factors-and-warning-signs/. Accessed 2021.
Preventing suicide: Fact sheet 2018. Centers for Disease Control and Prevention. https://www.cdc.gov/violenceprevention/suicide/index.html . Accessed 2021.
Gwinn, C. and Hellman, C. (2018). In Morgan James Publishing (Ed.), Hope Rising: How the Science of HOPE Can Change Your Life. New York.

Made in the USA
Middletown, DE
08 April 2022

63856061R00096